750+
HAND-DRAWN
EMBROIDERY
DESIGNS TO INSPIRE
YOUR STITCHES

Pen to Thread

SARAH WATSON

INTERWEAVE.
interweave.com

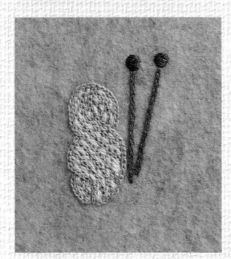

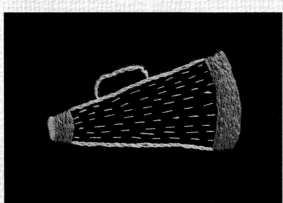

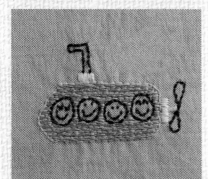

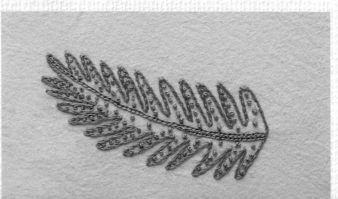

Contents

Hello!

I KNOW YOU'RE excited to delve into this book; I'm excited for you! Whether you're an old hand or a newcomer to embroidery, I know you will love this book.

I work as an illustrator and designer, and I love to create simple, whimsical line drawings of everyday things—from pizza to backpacks—often with a touch of make-believe, such as a mermaid or a unicorn, thrown in for good measure.

For this book, I have selected my absolute favorite motifs from the many I have drawn. As I hope you'll agree, they are imaginative and full of personality and range from tiny, superquick embroideries to large, intricate designs that may take a day or so to embroider. No matter what motif you choose, you can use my inspirational stitched examples to decide how simple or intricate you'd like yours to be. I've also included useful motifs such as frames, borders, and alphabets, and a section full of creative suggestions on where and how to use your finished embroideries.

In addition to motifs of all kinds, I've included some information about the basics, just in case you are new to embroidery. I discuss threads, fabrics, and essential stitch instructions, along with helpful step-by-step stitch diagrams.

Embroidery is a wonderful skill to have, a hobby that is relaxing and portable, and that results in a fantastic finished product. Writing this book has inspired me to be creative as often as I can, and I hope it does the same for you. So gather your threads, needles, and fabric, and get ready to stitch!

Getting Started: the Essentials

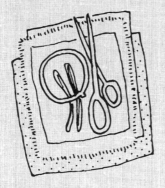

THERE IS A great deal of paraphernalia available for embroidery. If you're new to the craft, it can be overwhelming and a bit intimidating to walk into the embroidery aisle of your favorite store. Luckily, embroidery is a craft that you can start with some very basic tools. Then you can add other supplies and tools as you get more involved and gain experience. When I embroider, I usually use just the basics—fabric, thread, needle, and scissors. I love that embroidery can be so simple.

In this chapter, I'll introduce you to my favorite things—all the different types of fabrics and colorful threads that you'll use for your embroidery.

I'll also expand past the basic tools to introduce you to things such as hoops and transfer supplies that you can use when you embroider.

STITCH SAMPLER

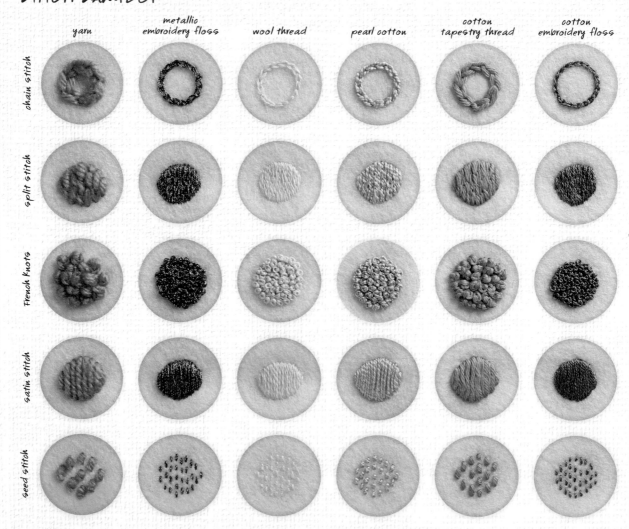

	yarn	metallic embroidery floss	wool thread	pearl cotton	cotton tapestry thread	cotton embroidery floss
chain stitch						
split stitch						
French knots						
satin stitch						
seed stitch						

threads

HOW DO YOU PICK THE RIGHT THREAD?

There are options galore out there, and each thread has a specific end use. The most commonly used threads for hand embroidery are stranded embroidery floss, pearl cotton, and crewel thread. If you feel like experimenting with non-traditional threads, you can also try sewing thread and yarn. They all have the same basic structure: a filament that can be threaded through a needle and pulled through fabric. When you get past the basics, though, they're all quite different. Aside from price, color selection, and availability, how do you know what's best for your project? To help you choose, I'll go over some of their qualities here.

EMBROIDERY FLOSS

Embroidery floss is usually made from cotton, with the exception of some specialty threads, such as metallic and nylon or polyester alternatives. It comes in a multitude of colors and is readily available. Typically, embroidery floss comes in a thickness of six strands, loosely twisted together. There are two- and four-strand embroidery threads available, as well as some that come in 100% wool or a wool/polyester blend. You can use as many strands as you like; they are easy to separate. If you've never worked with embroidery floss, try starting with three strands. Most of the motifs in this book work best when used with three strands of floss. This choice works well on anything from basic beginner embroidery to more intricate advanced work.

However, because you can work with anything from a single strand to all six strands, floss also works well for tiny projects up to very large ones. The delicacy of a single strand is good for tiny motifs, while the more strands you use, the bolder the designs become.

Along with a great variety of colors, embroidery floss also comes in metallic, neon, and glow-in-the-dark (a favorite of mine). I highly recommend giving all colors and types a try.

PEARL COTTON

Pearl cotton is usually found on lime-sized balls of thread and, less commonly, on a skein. Although pearl cotton is always available in specialty shops, you can also find it at larger craft stores as it becomes more and more popular. It is made up of twisted strands, like embroidery floss, but is non-divisible. So that makes it important that you choose the right size for your project. Pearl cotton is generally available in a handful of sizes, with size 3 being the thickest and size 12 the finest. Size 8 is generally what I've used throughout this book.

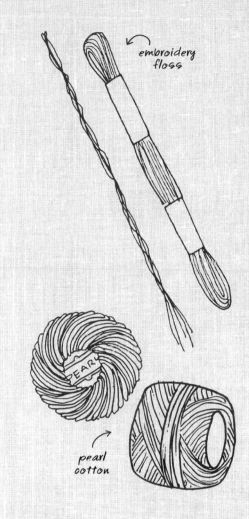

embroidery floss

pearl cotton

tip Lots of times I choose threads based on color or texture alone. If I see a type of thread that I've never seen before or that is in a color I know I won't find elsewhere, I go ahead and get it and then experiment with it. Sometimes it will work, and sometimes it won't. But I always know that if I've bought it because I love it, I'll be able to use it somewhere in my crafting, even if it doesn't work for embroidery.

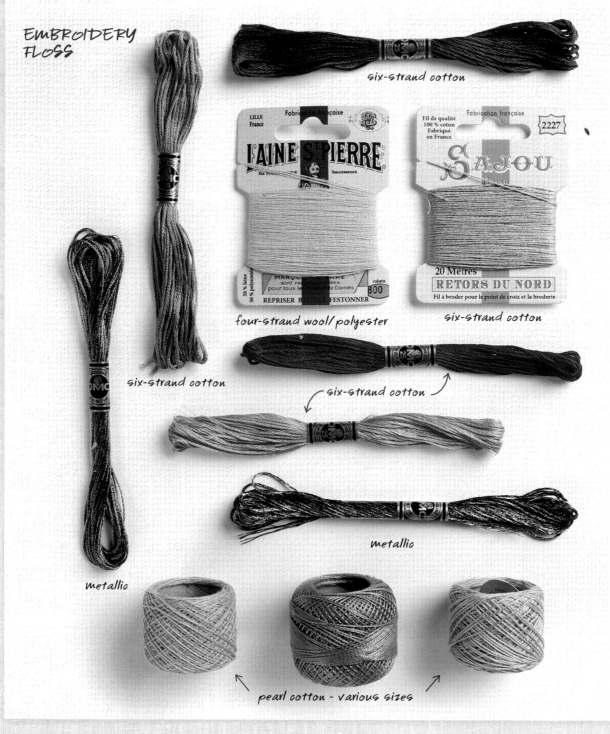

EMBROIDERY FLOSS

six-strand cotton

four-strand wool/ polyester

six-strand cotton

six-strand cotton

six-strand cotton

metallic

metallic

metallic

pearl cotton - various sizes

Pearl cotton has a lovely sheen to it, and the twist of the thread can add a nice texture to your embroidery. Just like embroidery floss, this is a very common thread for all levels of embroiderers, and it's useful for the majority of embroidery projects.

CREWEL THREAD

Crewelwork is a heavier, loftier type of embroidery, so remember that when looking at crewel thread. It is most commonly wool, two-ply and twisted, meaning its two strands cannot be separated. Because crewel thread is a bit heavier, it's best to avoid using it for tiny embroideries.

YARN, CROCHET, AND TAPESTRY THREAD

These three are great for adding texture and dimension to an embroidery. Crochet thread varies in sizes and can easily be confused with pearl cotton, because it is sold in the same cute little balls. It comes in varying sizes, but in general, it is thicker than pearl cotton and therefore works better for larger embroideries, or for details such as French knots or decorative individual stitches.

Yarn comes in many different weights (thicknesses), but basically it's pretty thick. Tapestry thread, available in cotton or wool, is about equal thickness, so I'll describe them together. I like to use yarn on larger-scale embroideries in single seed stitches (page 31) and for French knots (page 29). Be careful when working with yarn and tapestry thread, though. You're going to need to use a larger needle, and this will result in larger holes in your fabric, which makes mistakes harder to cover up. Burlap and loose-weave fabrics accommodate larger needles and thicker thread better.

SEWING THREAD

Because it is thin, ordinary sewing thread is good for stitching really nice subtle details, such as shading or fine lines, in your embroidery project. Or, when used as the sole thread choice for an embroidery, sewing thread can result in a very neat hand-drawn look. Work in a straight stitch or backstitch (page 26) and keep your stitch length short for better results (Long stitches can snag and easily break.) If you can't find the right color of sewing thread, just use a single strand of embroidery floss.

A fun way to experiment with sewing thread is to choose three to five different colored threads, cut them the same length, and combine them by slightly twisting them together. Use them as you would embroidery floss. You might need to use a needle threader (page 17) to get all the strands through the eye of the needle, but the effect is worth the effort! It's like creating your own unique, multicolored embroidery floss.

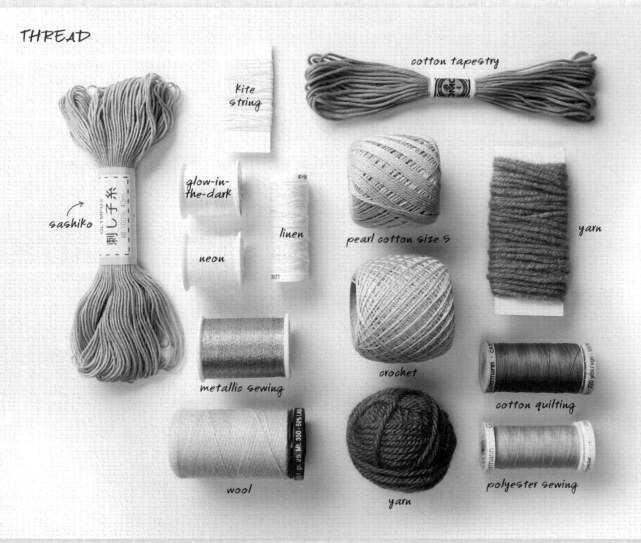

THREAD

sashiko

Kite string

cotton tapestry

glow-in-the-dark

neon

linen

pearl cotton size 5

yarn

metallic sewing

crochet

cotton quilting

wool

yarn

polyester sewing

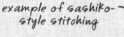

tip When you're working with a new thread, it's always important to do a test-drive first. I keep a scrap patch of fabric nearby when I'm working, so that I can test out a new thread before trying it on my actual embroidery. If you use it long enough, this scrap will become a beautiful "drop cloth" of stitches, colors, and texture. Try some of the threads I've talked about for a new outlook when you are choosing your next embroidery thread.

OTHER THREADS

Never be afraid to try something new. Threads come in different materials including linen, wool, and synthetics. I love working with glow-in-the-dark thread, in place of white or cream. It adds a nice unexpected detail to your work, and used in a piece you give as a gift, it can provide quite a surprise! Metallic thread can be very tricky and a bit frustrating to work with at times, but it will sparkle and shine in your finished work. It can twist or break easily, so it's best to work with short cuts of metallic thread.

Traditional sashiko thread doesn't need to be restricted to traditional sashiko designs! Use it as you would pearl cotton or crochet yarn. You can also layer a nice sashiko pattern as a background to your freehand embroidery. It makes a wonderful mix and match of styles.

When working with any thread, it's best to cut a length of thread that is manageable for you and that won't tangle. A length of 18 to 30 inches (45.5 to 76 cm) works well for me, so start with that length, and eventually you will find what you are comfortable with. Smooth a cut piece out with your fingers to avoid twists when working. If your thread does twist, hold your embroidery up and let the needle drop and spin until the twist is out. Personally, I like to work with a complete skein and pull and cut lengths as I need them. But, if you are interested in learning how to cut your full skein into equal lengths, refer to the DMC website, listed in Resources (page 149).

example of sashiko-style stitching

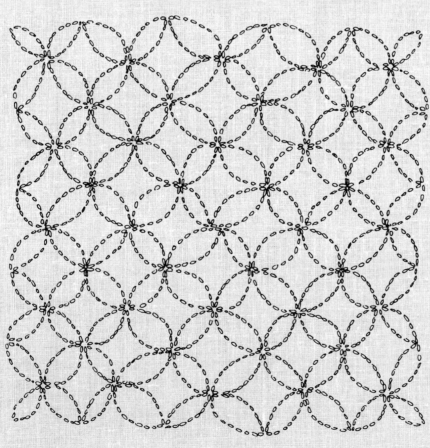

fabric

A WORLD OF OPTIONS

The first thing most people think of when choosing what base to embroider on is flat-weave fabric such as cotton. Flat-weave fabric is beautiful to embroider on, but as with thread, there is a world of other options. Some of my favorite looks come from using repurposed clothing, fashion fabrics, laminates, lace, and even paper. They may take a little experimentation to get the hang of, but the effects are wonderful. Here are some of my favorites, and why you might, or might not, want to use them. To see swatches of these various fabric types, look at the Materials Sampler (pages 12–13).

WOVEN FABRIC

Woven fabrics are any that are made of a warp and weft, meaning vertical and horizontal threads that are woven over and under each other to create a fabric. When working with woven fabric, you'll want to choose something that has enough body to hold up under your stitching. Woven fabric has many subcategories, so I'll describe three basic weights I like—light, medium, and heavy.

Lightweight: muslin + quilting cotton

About as basic as you can get, unbleached muslin is great not only for its price but also for its raw quality. The neutral color of muslin allows you to use vibrant thread-color schemes. Quilting cotton is available in a splendid array of solid colors. Subtle, small-scale prints can also make really nice ground fabric for embroidery. Just make sure they aren't so bold that they draw attention away from your embroidery. Both unbleached natural muslin and quilting cotton have a beautiful look, but they can be a bit flimsy and lightweight, so make sure to add a layer of interfacing or other stabilizer behind them.

Medium weight: linen + shirting

Both of these are used plentifully throughout this book. Linen and shirting are a bit sturdier and have more texture than quilting cotton. I find this weight really nice to embroider on, because it holds up better to tight stitches and makes mistakes less obvious. However, their textured surface limits you to using tissue paper to transfer your designs to these fabrics (see Transfer Techniques & Supplies, page 18), so take that into consideration when planning an embroi-

dery. These fabrics are great to embroider on and turn into items such as purses, clothing, or home décor items such as throw pillows.

Heavyweight: canvas + denim

These fabrics are great for making embroidered patches and badges. Pushing a needle through thick fabrics like these can get a bit tough, so use a thimble. Transferring your pattern using a light source likely won't work with these, because they'll be too thick to see through. So try your hand at the tissue paper, iron on, or carbon paper transfer methods described in Transfer Techniques & Supplies (page 18).

FELT: WOOL + SYNTHETIC

Felt is a nonwoven fabric, meaning that is does not have a warp and weft like woven fabrics. Instead, it is created from matted fibers. Traditional felt is made of wool, but now you'll also find it in 100% polyester, blends of rayon and

Label swatches of fabrics you will want to use again, so it's easy to go back and get more.

fabric: _____
season: _____
year: _____
purchased: _____

wool, bamboo, and blends with cotton scrim. No matter the fiber content, felts come in a range of colors and thicknesses. Synthetic felt often has a loftier side and a smoother side. I find it easier to embroider on the smoother side.

The thickness and texture of felt is very forgiving. If your stitches are too tight, felt doesn't shrink and pucker like woven fabrics. And if you need to remove stitches, the holes will rarely show through afterward. However, small stitches or thinner threads can get lost in the loft of some felt, so make sure to do a test first if you're thinking of using a thin thread or short stitches. Tissue paper is a great transfer technique (page 19) to use with felt.

NONTRADITIONAL FABRIC

This is my name for anything with stretch, or with an unfamiliar texture—such as burlap, faux leather, knits, laminated cotton, and vinyl—which can be difficult to transfer and embroider on. But I like these types of fabrics because they can offer unique color, texture, or sheen. My quick fix for stretchy or slinky fabrics is to use a lightweight fusible interfacing. This will result in a sturdy fabric that can easily be embroidered on. Be careful when using an iron on "mystery fabrics," some of which can melt under the heat of the iron. I suggest that you use a press cloth to protect your fabric, iron, and ironing board. Always test on a scrap of your fabric before pressing the entire piece that you plan to embroider.

For fabric with a rough texture or open weave, such as burlap, use the tissue paper transfer technique (page 19). When working with

MATERIALS SAMPLER

denim chambray

canvas

linen

cotton duck cloth

linen

muslin

burlap

quilters' cotton

burlap

cotton shirting

ripstop nylon

woven cotton plaid

foil paper

printed cotton

wool felt

recycled cotton shirting

metallic vinyl

printed cotton

felt

recycled woven cotton shirting

faux leather

printed cotton

synthetic felt

doubleweave cotton

jersey

patterned paper

synthetic felt

woven cotton plaid

jersey

kraft paper

tip You can make a lighter weight fabric sturdier by adding a layer of interfacing or stabilizer to the back, or even by cutting your fabric twice as wide and folding it in half to double the thickness. Adding interfacing or another layer of fabric is also a great way to make sure that none of the stitches and knots on the back of your embroidery show through on the front. I know my embroidery backs can get out of hand sometimes, so I almost always work with a layer of interfacing to hide rogue stitches and knots. When adding interfacing, always make sure that you match your interfacing with the fabric color—white interfacing with light-colored fabrics and dark interfacing with dark-colored fabrics.

Secondhand and thrift stores can be sources for some great fabrics. I love fabric from the men's section in secondhand stores.

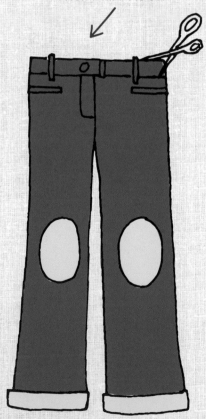

a solid material such as vinyl or faux leather, carefully plan your colors and stitches before you make them, just as you would with paper. Then stitch them carefully, too. Holes in solid materials can't be removed, so they will show in your final work.

PAPER

I first started stitching on paper with my sewing machine. There is something about the needle poking through the paper that made me want to try to embroider on it, too! It doesn't work for all embroidery: if you are stitching a lot of details, you'll poke too many needle holes, and the paper will just fall apart. But simple outlined embroideries can be great on paper. Choose paper that is relatively sturdy, such as kraft paper or cardstock. Use tape to keep your thread ends in check on the back side. If you want the back to look clean, tape another piece of paper neatly on the back side, using double-sided tape. To transfer your design motif to the paper, simply trace it with a pencil or print it out on your printer. If you use a printer, remember that the ink is permanent, so you will need to cover it completely with thread.

FABRIC, NEW + OLD

I love fabric. Whether I'm walking through a fabric store, a craft store, or a secondhand clothing shop, I'm always excited and looking for great textiles. What makes a fabric great is different for each person. It can be the color, pattern, texture, feel, or a combination.

New fabric

When you select a brand-new fabric, always wash, dry, and iron it before starting an embroidery project. Not all new fabric will shrink, but it's best to be careful.

Anytime I buy a new fabric that I know I'll want to use again, I cut a small swatch and label it with the brand, color, and place where I bought it. This makes it easy for me to go back and get more if I need it. If I've run out and can't find the original fabric anywhere, I can still take the swatch with me and try to find as close a match as possible.

Recycled fabric

Secondhand and thrift stores can be sources for some great fabrics. I love fabric from the men's section in secondhand stores. This is a great place to find unique colors and patterns. Next time you're making a special embroidery project, try purchasing a used article of clothing, such as a men's button-down shirt or lightweight pants, and repurposing the fabric.

If you choose recycled fabric for embroidery, here are a few important things to remember.

SIZE. Make sure you are providing yourself enough material to finish your project. If you're framing your embroidery, using it in a quilt or as a patch, or incorporating it into a sewing pattern, this can be very clear-cut. But if you're not certain what the end use for your embroidery will be, you'll need to make sure you have enough fabric to play around with if you do decide to make something out of it.

STAINS AND HOLES. Stains and holes in the larger sections of fabric, like the back and front panels of a man's button-down shirt, will drastically cut down on usable material, so always check for those before purchasing.

WORN-OUT FABRIC. Try to find a garment that hasn't been worn to death (unless, of course, that's what you're looking for). Fabrics that have a noticeable pill (those balls on fabric blends that result from too much wear and laundering), or that have worn through, will show in your final product. You don't want to spend a lot of time on a beautiful embroidery, only to find that your base fabric looks tattered or unclean.

Take home your newly purchased article of clothing and wash it using regular detergent, along with any stain fighter if needed. Afterward, dry and iron it. I find it best to completely deconstruct the article of clothing right when I start working with it. Cut everything out along the seams and salvage anything you can, such as buttons, zippers, pockets, or collars, for other projects. Neatly fold your fresh "vintage" fabric and store it along with the rest of your stash. Because these pieces are irregular in size and shape, it's nice to keep them organized in a shoebox, in zippered plastic storage bags, or in other compartmentalized storage.

EMBROIDERING ON READY-MADE OBJECTS

Backpacks, clothing, and linens such as tablecloths, towels, and pillowcases are some items that I love to embroider directly on. These usually have just a single layer of fabric, and the reverse side is rarely visible, making them ideal for embroidery. They are usually made of one of the fabrics I've previously described, so keep that in mind when selecting a ready-made object to work on.

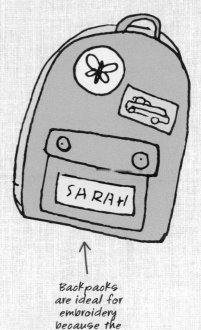

Backpacks are ideal for embroidery because the reverse side is not visible.

---

tip A fun way to add texture or sparkle to your embroidery is to layer a piece of mesh or netting on top of your fabric, so you're working with two layers of fabric. Baste the netting in place or sandwich it along with your base cloth in the embroidery hoop to keep it in place. Try water-soluble stabilizer when transferring designs to these odd fabrics.

On the item, decide where you'd like to embroider, and transfer your design as you would on a loose piece of fabric (see Transfer Techniques & Supplies, page 18). If you can use an embroidery hoop, that might help you maneuver the object while working. For bulky or oddly shaped objects such as backpacks, just go straight ahead and work. After finishing your embroidery, if you'd like to protect your stitches and knots, or want a clean reverse side, iron on a layer of adhesive interfacing or use double-sided adhesive interfacing to attach a layer of fabric. Try a variety of transfer techniques for ready-made objects.

embroiderer's toolbox

IT'S GOOD TO have all of your embroidery supplies in one easy-to-find location. If you're a sewer as well, it's easy enough to keep it together with all of your other sewing supplies. But if you're just taking on embroidery, or if you plan on moving your supplies around, it's nice to have everything in one spot. (Embroidery is a great vacation activity, good for long car rides, relaxing at a campsite, or sitting in front of a fire with a cup of hot chocolate!) Here are a few more supplies—including the basic needles and scissors—that you might want to put together and keep in a specific place.

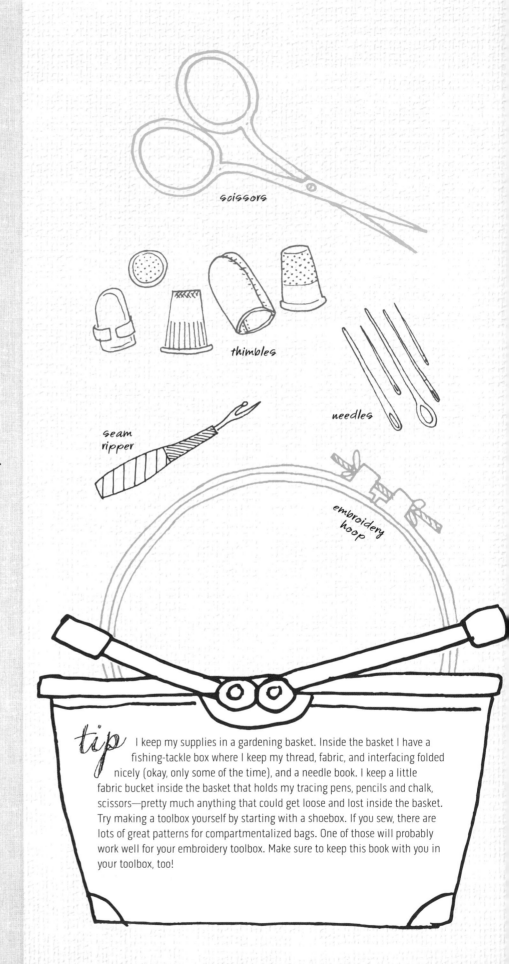

scissors

thimbles

needles

seam ripper

embroidery hoop

tip   I keep my supplies in a gardening basket. Inside the basket I have a fishing-tackle box where I keep my thread, fabric, and interfacing folded nicely (okay, only some of the time), and a needle book. I keep a little fabric bucket inside the basket that holds my tracing pens, pencils and chalk, scissors—pretty much anything that could get loose and lost inside the basket. Try making a toolbox yourself by starting with a shoebox. If you sew, there are lots of great patterns for compartmentalized bags. One of those will probably work well for your embroidery toolbox. Make sure to keep this book with you in your toolbox, too!

NEEDLES

There are a wide variety of needles out there. I'm a bit of a rebel, and my basic rule is: if I can fit the thread through the needle's eye, I'll use it. But if you're the rule-following type, there are some rules for which needles to use in specific situations.

Embroidery needles are made especially for embroidery, with larger eyeholes to accommodate embroidery thread, and are usually of medium length.

Tapestry needles, although used for a type of embroidery, are a bit more specific. The tip of a tapestry needle is less sharp than others, making it ideal for looser weave fabrics. These needles could be a good choice for embroidering a large-scale design on those fabrics.

Quilter's sharps work well with sewing thread, they're shorter in length, and they're extra sharp because they're usually used for stitching through all the layers of a quilt.

Choose the length of the needle based on the work you are doing. A longer needle will be helpful if you are doing a running stitch, and you want to get a number of stitches onto your needle before pulling it through the fabric. And I find shorter needles helpful when stitching French knots.

I like to keep a selection of needles handy in a felt needle book.

By the way, needle threaders can really cut down on the frustration level if you have a hard time threading your needle. You simply insert the tip of the threader into the eye of the needle and then run your thread or embroidery floss through the opening in the threader and pull the thread through. Then, remove the threader. Voila!

SCISSORS

It's great to have some options on scissors. Don't worry if you're just getting started and have only one pair. As long as they cut, they'll do! But here are some useful types.

Fabric scissors or pinking shears are nice to have to cut your pieces of fabric. Fabric scissors are generally supersharp. Dedicated sewers guard them heavily to be used only on fabric because that keeps them at their sharpest.

I like to keep a pair of small pointed scissors for snipping threads, cutting intricate areas or removing stitches, if needed.

For cutting patterns, carbon paper, or anything else, a regular pair of household scissors works fine.

All of these types of scissors are easy to find at your local sewing or craft store. If you can't find specific fabric scissors, label your sharpest regular scissors with a ribbon tied to the handle, to be used only for fabric, and they'll likely stay in good shape.

THIMBLE

These are great to have if you're stubborn like me, and you keep pushing your needle through too many layers of fabric or a knot. I personally don't use one because I seem to work fine without them. There are many types of thimbles—leather thimbles, metal thimbles, gel thimbles, and even sticky thimbles. Borrow some from a friend or try them on at the store to see what you like best.

Place the thimble on the finger you use to push the needle through fabric to keep your finger from getting callused by the eye end of the needle.

SEAM RIPPER

These are nice if you're prone to mistakes or changes of heart. (It's okay to make mistakes—we all do.) If you find that you need to tear out some stitches, use one of these. Sometimes, I also use a fine-tip utility knife, such as an X-Acto knife, which works just about as well.

RULER

I keep a 6-inch (15 cm) ruler and a measuring tape on hand at all times. These are just plain useful, no matter what you're doing.

EMBROIDERY HOOP

I don't always use an embroidery hoop; I like to be able to feel the tension of the thread against the fabric in my hands. This doesn't mean I never use one. Embroidery hoops are useful if you constantly find yourself stitching too tightly, ending up with bunched-up fabric around your design. They come in all shapes and sizes, in wood, metal, and plastic. Plastic hoops are nice because there is no danger that they'll mar your fabric. I find it easiest to work with smaller hoops (around 5 inches in diameter) because I can stretch my fingers toward the center of the hoop and guide while I stitch.

transfer techniques + supplies

TRANSFERRING YOUR chosen embroidery motif from paper to fabric is that one step you need to make the jump from a pile of supplies to an embroidery ready to be worked on. Often, I find myself procrastinating just because of this step. Luckily there are some painless, easy transfer techniques out there that will have you embroidering in no time! Here, I review my favorites.

TRANSFER TOOLS

PENCIL. Regular lead pencils are nice to use for transferring designs. The markings they make are light, so if you don't completely cover them with stitches or can't erase them all, you probably won't notice in the end. White-colored pencils can work well on dark fabric.

DRESSMAKER'S CHALK PENCIL. I use this to transfer designs onto dark fabrics, where a regular pencil or pen won't show up. Sometimes, I even use an opaque white ballpoint pen. But remember that this, like a normal pen, is permanent.

EMBROIDERY TRANSFER PEN. These pens usually come in a blue color and are reasonably priced. They transfer just like a marker, and after completing the embroidery, you can remove them with a damp cloth or cold-water rinse. But they do have their drawbacks. If you live in a very humid environment, or you don't plan to finish your embroidery in a short period of time, the design can fade away before you have a chance to do all of the stitching. Make sure you've allotted plenty of time to complete your masterpiece if you're using one of these pens.

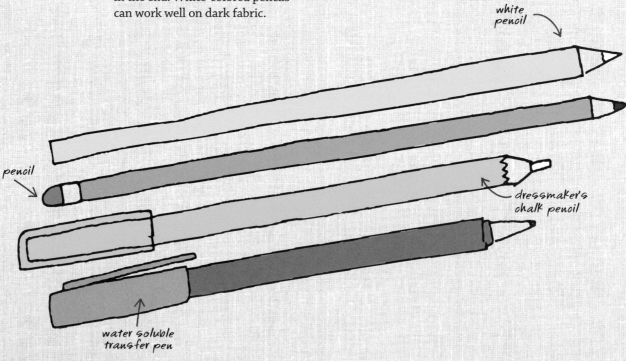

white pencil

pencil

dressmaker's chalk pencil

water soluble transfer pen

tip Before using water-soluble stabilizer, make sure all of your threads are colorfast. A simple way to test them is to make a running stitch of each color on a piece of fabric. (Use your beautiful "drop cloth" test piece, see page 10!) Submerge the fabric in warm water until the threads are soaked. If there's no color bleeding, you're good to go.

You may find it easier to leave small details until after you have torn out the paper, which is fine, as long as you can remember where they go. Keep the master copy of your motif nearby for easy reference. If you're working on an embroidery and happen to accidentally tear off the paper completely (don't worry, it happens all the time!), just retrace and replace on top of your embroidery, making sure to align it with what you have already stitched.

TISSUE PAPER

I do most of my embroidery on textured fabric and felt. I love the depth that they give to threadwork and the way the needle feels gliding through the fabric. With their wonderful texture and weight, the best transfer technique to use with these fabrics is tissue paper. Simply take a piece of smooth white tissue paper, trace your chosen motif with pencil or ballpoint pen, and pin or baste the tissue paper on top of your base fabric.

Begin stitching just as you would without the paper there. Stitch your complete design, running your needle from the wrong side of the fabric, up to the top through the tissue paper and then back to the wrong side. Gently tear away the paper in small pieces, being careful not to tug at your stitches. When you have finished, use tweezers or a blunt needle to pick out any bits of tissue paper you aren't able to remove with your fingers.

WATER-SOLUBLE STABILIZER

Although I prefer tissue paper because I always have it on hand, water-soluble stabilizer is an amazing transfer material. You can find it at most craft and sewing stores.

Trace your design onto the stabilizer with a pen or pencil and use as you would tissue paper. Some of these products allow you to place them in a printer's paper tray and print a design from your computer. If you are printing from the computer, save scrap pieces to use with the pen/tracing method. Baste or pin your design onto your fabric and embroider as usual. For the final step, submerge your embroidery in lukewarm water, and the stabilizer will disintegrate. You may need to change the water once to get all of it out.

TRACING WITH A LIGHT SOURCE

Next to tracing onto tissue paper, this is the method I use the most. I tend to do things the simplest possible way. This is super easy and can be used on many fabrics. Dark fabrics can be tough, but I find that with a bright light and a lightweight fabric, it's still manageable.

Tape or pin a paper copy of your chosen motif to the back side of your fabric. Then tape the fabric to a bright, sunny window or to a light box. If neither of these is available, try setting a glass baking pan in your lap with a flashlight underneath. This might seem a little odd, but it works! Use a transfer pencil, pen, or chalk to trace your design onto your fabric.

CARBON TRANSFER PAPER

Dressmaker's carbon paper is thin paper with one side covered in transfer material. It comes in a variety of colors, so you can use it on light and dark fabrics. It will work best on smooth-textured fabrics. Sandwich a piece of carbon paper between your motif and your fabric, with the inked side of the paper facing the fabric, and tape or pin it in place. Use an empty ballpoint pen, pointed wooden skewer, or sharp colored pencil to trace over your design. Sometimes it can be hard to see where you've already traced, so using something like a colored pencil can give you an advantage in those circumstances. After you have traced your design, save your carbon paper. One piece is usually good for a couple of transfers. If there is any residue left on the fabric after you have done your embroidery, try brushing it off with a stiff, dry paintbrush.

IRON-ON TRANSFER PAPER

Simply print your design onto this paper, trim to size, and use your iron, following the manufacturer's instructions, to transfer the design onto your fabric. Keep in mind this very important detail: iron-on transfer designs will be a mirror image when you flip them over and iron them on. So make sure to always reverse your design before transferring it. These types of transfers create permanent lines, so you will need to be careful to cover up the whole design with stitching.

There are also hot-iron transfer markers and pencils that allow you to draw your design and then iron on the markings. Although I don't like using these myself, some people do.

Tape the fabric to a bright, sunny window or to a light box. If neither of these is available, try setting a glass baking pan in your lap with a flashlight underneath.

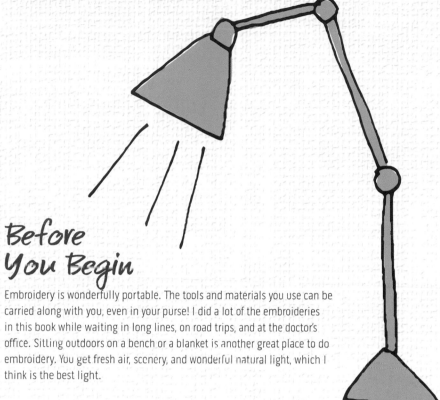

Before You Begin

Embroidery is wonderfully portable. The tools and materials you use can be carried along with you, even in your purse! I did a lot of the embroideries in this book while waiting in long lines, on road trips, and at the doctor's office. Sitting outdoors on a bench or a blanket is another great place to do embroidery. You get fresh air, scenery, and wonderful natural light, which I think is the best light.

It is very easy to strain your eyes when embroidering, so always make sure you have good light. This is not only for the care of your eyes, but also for your work. Colors can be misleading in dim light. It can be all too easy to think you've continued to stitch with white thread, when in fact you are using off-white. (See if you can find the embroideries in the book where I made this mistake—there are a few!) If you can't manage to work during daylight hours, or are stuck inside, just make sure you are sitting in a well-lit area.

Before you do any embroidery, make sure your hands are clean. This may seem like obvious advice, but far too often I've cuddled up with a cup of coffee or a snack and an embroidery project, only to end up with a beautiful embroidery and a mess on my fabric! Make sure to keep your hands free of food and oils, including hand cream, which can transfer onto fabrics.

tip Take a break every now and then! Handiwork is fun, but rest, exercise, and stretching are important. Get up and take a walk if you're working on a long project. It will invigorate you and get you ready to start back in.

Embroidery Basics

NOW THAT YOU have your tools and materials together, it's time to make some decisions and start stitching! What's that, you say? You're not sure which stitch, color, or motif to use? No worries—I've got you covered. Check out the following section for a quick stitch guide and for ideas about where and how to use the designs.

If you're an old hand at embroidery, you might be able to breeze past these next few pages. Go, you! Get a project going! For the rest of us, there are some great tips for beginners, and later on, some wonderful creative advice for all levels.

Hoop it

To use an embroidery hoop, loosen the nut and bolt so that the outer hoop comes off. Set it aside. Place your fabric (with interfacing basted on the back) on top of your inner hoop, with the design centered in the middle. Now place the larger hoop on top. It should fit over easily; if not, loosen the nut a bit more. As you tighten the bolt, gently pull the edges of your fabric taut. Make sure not to warp your fabric. Pull evenly on all sides as you tighten the bolt and push the outer hoop over the inner hoop.

Setting up

MAKING THE FIRST CUT

If you're not creating an embroidery that needs to be a specific size, for a specific project, you should usually prepare a piece of fabric that allows for at least a 3-inch (7.6 cm) border around the edges of your finished embroidery. This ensures that you can frame or sew your embroidery into a finished product when you are done. To keep the outside edges of your fabric from fraying, be sure to either cut the outside edges with pinking shears or zigzag stitch around the outside edges. If using interfacing, cut it the same size and baste it on the wrong side around the outside edges. (Make sure you have already transferred your embroidery before basting on the interfacing.)

tip I rarely cut the correct length of thread, and I usually end up with a remnant of thread on my needle when I am done with one color. If this piece is large enough to be used again, I often save it for later use. (I consider anything longer than 4 or 5 inches [10 or 12.5 cm] reusable, even if only for a few stitches, but beginners might be more comfortable starting with a longer length—such as 10 to 12 inches [25.5 to 30.5 cm].) I always make sure to knot the end of my thread before I put it away. This way, when I go to thread my needle with the scrap piece of thread, I know I'll be pulling it in the right direction—and a knot is already in place. Keep a small container to hold your scrap thread. A drawstring bag or small box works well.

STARTING & ENDING YOUR THREAD

When pulling floss or other threads with twisted strands off a skein, it is important to make sure you start from the correct end. Pull skeins have an end thread (the "original end") that will enable you to keep pulling lengths from your skein without knotting up the floss or thread. Floss and threads are twisted in a certain direction, which allows them to run through fabric more easily. Pulling the wrong end of the thread from the skein won't be the end of the world, but it will result in more twisting and knotting.

On a skein, find one end of the thread and gently pull. If it tangles up, then you've probably pulled from the wrong end, so try the other one. (This isn't an exact science, so don't get too frustrated!) Once I've found the original end, I like to tie a knot on the other loose end of the skein, to remind me not to pull from it. Neatly cut a length of about 18 to 30 inches (45.5 to 76 cm).

If you plan to separate the strands, hold the original end of your cut length while you pull out the desired number of strands. Pull them out one at a time. Be sure to keep track of the original end of the strands, so that you know which end to put through the needle. When you have your desired number of strands pulled, combine them at the original end and smooth them into a single thread. When you are ready to thread your needle, pick up the original end and pass it through the needle first.

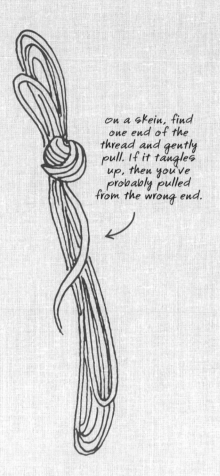

On a skein, find one end of the thread and gently pull. If it tangles up, then you've probably pulled from the wrong end.

QUILTER'S KNOT →

If you're a handquilter, you likely know this technique very well. I wasted a lot of time struggling with knots until I learned about this one. Who knew it was so easy? To create a knot at the end of your thread, simply thread your needle, and with the end of your thread facing toward the point of your needle, wrap the thread around the needle three times **(FIG. 1)**. Using your index finger and thumb, gently pinch the wrapped section of the needle and pull the needle through the thread wraps to the end of your thread

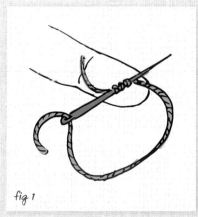

fig 1

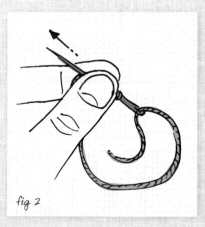

fig 2

(FIG. 2). The wrapped portion of your thread will knot on its own upon reaching the end of the line.

AWAY WASTE KNOT ↓

Knots on the back of your embroidery can make it lumpy. A nice way to avoid this is to use an "away waste knot." This knot is "away" at a small distance, a few inches, from your first stitch. Make your quilter's knot as usual, but when starting your embroidery, insert your needle at A **(FIG. 3)** so that the knot is on the front of your fabric, a few inches (5 to 10 cm) away from your design. Complete your embroidery as usual, making sure not to embroider over the waste knot and the loose thread. When you're finished with that thread, "waste" the knot by snipping it off close to the fabric **(FIG. 4)**. With the length of thread that is left, thread it through your needle, then stitch through about 1 inch (2.5 cm) of your previous stitches on the wrong side **(FIG. 5 AND FIG. 6)**. Then do the same in the opposite direction **(FIG. 7)** and snip your thread **(FIG. 8)**.

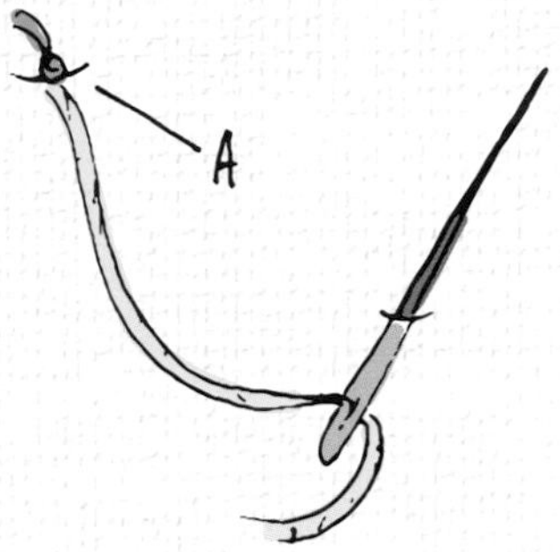

fig 3

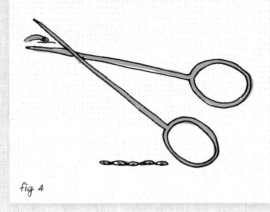

fig 4

fig 5

fig 6

fig 7

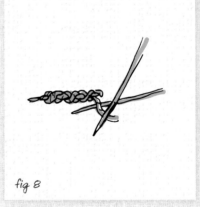

fig 8

Stitching through to finish

The best way to finish your thread is to stitch it through the back of your design as you did in the last steps of the away waste knot (figures 5 through 8 above). (If you sew, think of how you do a short backstitch to anchor your thread at the beginning and end.) After you have finished your embroidery, end with your thread and needle on the wrong side. Stitch through about 1 inch (2.5 cm) of previous stitches, do the same in the opposite direction, and snip off your thread.

basic stitches

Over the years embroiderers have developed many, many stitches, some of which are quite ornate. However, when you have an interesting motif and colors you love, you can go a long way in embroidery with only a handful of simple stitches in your arsenal. I rarely stray away from the stitches I show you in this section. After you have mastered these, see Resources (page 149) if you want to learn more.

RUNNING STITCH →

Use to outline a motif, to add the illusion of shading, or in multiple rows for a light filling.

EXAMPLES: Clock , Tape measure

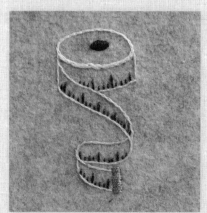

The running stitch is the simplest of simple stitches. If you've ever used a needle and thread before, chances are you already know how to do a running stitch.

Simply pull the needle and thread up through the fabric at A **(FIG. 9)** from the wrong side, and down through the fabric at B **(FIG. 10)**, and continue in this fashion **(FIG. 11)**. Try to keep your stitches of similar lengths on the front and back. Once you are comfortable with this stitch, try making more than one stitch at a time, running your needle through the fabric a few times before pulling your thread through. It's a nice time-saver.

Running stitches can be shortened quite a bit, as well as lengthened to a certain point, but you're not going to want to make them too long, or they could droop or get snagged. Experiment on your "drop cloth" (page 10) with short stitches or with varying lengths for fun.

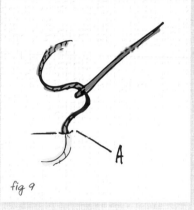

fig 9

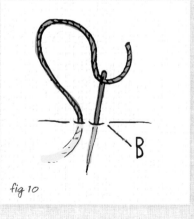

fig 10

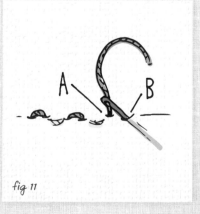

fig 11

BACKSTITCH ↘

Use to outline a motif, create borders, and, when lined up closely in rows, for filling.

EXAMPLES: Birdcage, Piñata

The backstitch is another simple stitch. It can be done in a smooth motion that keeps your stitching going quickly, but if you have trouble with it at first, don't feel bad about breaking the motion into individual steps. Often when I am working around the edges of a motif or curves, I break my backstitch down into single movements.

Insert the needle from the wrong side at A **(FIG. 12)** and pull the thread through. Reinsert the needle at B, and, one stitch length past B, bring it back out at C **(FIG. 13)**. Make sure your needle exits along the pattern line you are working on. After pulling your needle and thread completely through, you'll see that you will now have to go "back" to finish your stitch, hence the name "backstitch." Reinsert the needle at B **(FIG. 14)**. Come up again at C, which has now become your new A, and continue in this manner **(FIG. 15)**.

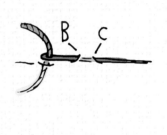

fig 12

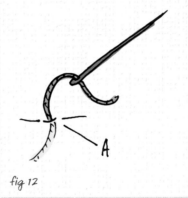

fig 13

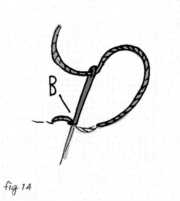

fig 14

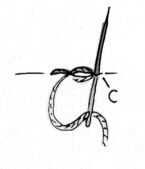

fig 15

SATIN STITCH →

Use to solidly fill in areas of various shapes in a motif.

EXAMPLES: Key, Lightning bolt

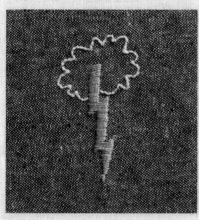

The satin stitch is an elegant, professional-looking stitch. You stitch from edge to edge of a shape, such as a leaf, using close parallel stitches. It takes a little practice to make the stitches perfectly smooth, but keep at it; it's worth it. For beginners, it is easiest to start with satin stitches in small areas, so that you can get the feel of how the thread will sit on top of your fabric once it is finished.

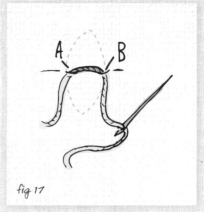

fig 16

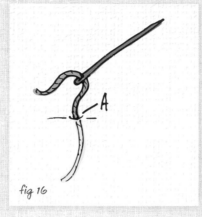

fig 17

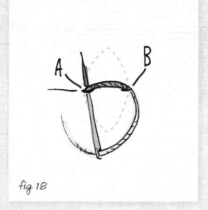

fig 18

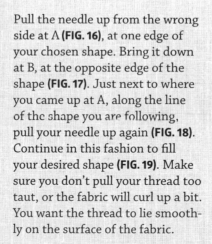

fig 19

Pull the needle up from the wrong side at A **(FIG. 16)**, at one edge of your chosen shape. Bring it down at B, at the opposite edge of the shape **(FIG. 17)**. Just next to where you came up at A, along the line of the shape you are following, pull your needle up again **(FIG. 18)**. Continue in this fashion to fill your desired shape **(FIG. 19)**. Make sure you don't pull your thread too taut, or the fabric will curl up a bit. You want the thread to lie smoothly on the surface of the fabric.

After you have a good feel for how the stitch works, start experimenting with it in larger areas. If you are having a hard time lining up the edges of your satin stitch, do a quick backstitch (page 26) or split stitch (page 28) around the outline of your motif first, to help guide you around the edges. Satin-stitch over the line of backstitches or split stitches for a smoother shape.

You can make satin stitches long or short to fill an area, but don't push it too far. If you make the stitches too long, they may loosen or sag. You will learn in your own time when it's best to fill a larger space using a split stitch instead of a satin stitch.

SPLIT STITCH ↘

Use to create a smooth, slightly raised outline around a motif, or to create a thick filling for any design shape.

EXAMPLES: Eagle, Bon Voyage

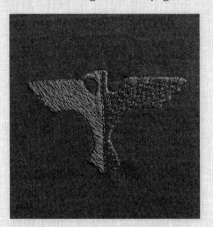

The split stitch is my favorite. Try using this stitch in place of the satin stitch for large areas you want to fill. It is much more forgiving than the satin stitch, and it fills in areas very thickly because it overlaps itself a little bit. With the split stitch, it's also easy to go back and add in a few extra stitches if you feel you've spaced out rows of stitches too far.

The split stitch works best with stranded thread, such as embroidery floss, because you'll be inserting your needle between strands of the floss, splitting it. When you're working around corners, a longer split stitch can begin to look jagged, so shorten your stitch

a bit to create a smooth line. Or do as I often do—just switch to a backstitch. (No one will notice the difference.)

Bring the needle up from the wrong side of the fabric at A and then down at B and pull the thread through to the wrong side of the fabric **(FIG. 20)**. Make sure the stitch you have just made is pulled through completely. Next, bring the needle up at C, coming up through the middle of your previous stitch and between the strands of your thread, splitting it **(FIG. 21)**. Pull the needle and thread through to the front completely. Continue **(FIG. 22)**.

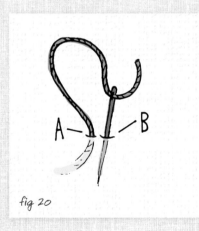

fig 20

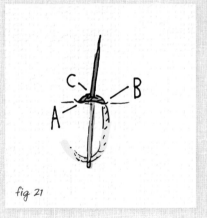

fig 21

fig 22

FRENCH KNOT →

Use individually to make dots or a nice, bumpy outline, and in clusters for flowers and for a fun-filled texture inside a shape… and so much more.

EXAMPLES: Poodle, Jar

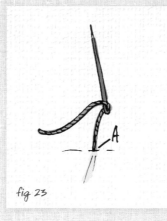

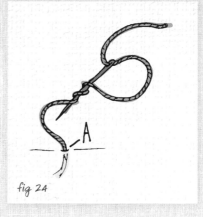

fig 23

fig 24

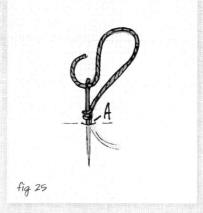

fig 25

Bring the needle up from the wrong side at A **(FIG. 23)**. Holding the thread taut and starting at the needle's midpoint, wrap the thread two or more times around the needle **(FIG. 24)**. Insert the needle back into the fabric at A **(FIG. 25)**, continuing to hold the thread taut near the knot as you gently pull the needle straight down, all the way through the fabric, until your knot is formed on the surface of the fabric.

The French knot is very versatile, and it can add a lot of interest to your embroidery, either individually or in clusters. Once you're comfortable with making French knots, experiment by wrapping the thread around the needle more times if you are using thin thread or fewer wraps for thicker thread, to create different-sized knots.

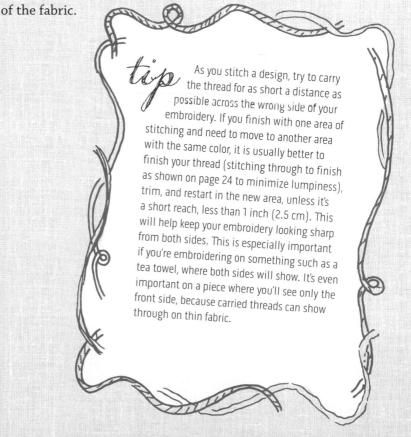

tip As you stitch a design, try to carry the thread for as short a distance as possible across the wrong side of your embroidery. If you finish with one area of stitching and need to move to another area with the same color, it is usually better to finish your thread (stitching through to finish as shown on page 24 to minimize lumpiness), trim, and restart in the new area, unless it's a short reach, less than 1 inch (2.5 cm). This will help keep your embroidery looking sharp from both sides. This is especially important if you're embroidering on something such as a tea towel, where both sides will show. It's even important on a piece where you'll see only the front side, because carried threads can show through on thin fabric.

CHAIN STITCH ↘

Use as a filler or to outline a motif. A tiny chain stitch makes a very special-looking outline stitch. Or use an individual stitch to create flowers or leaves.

EXAMPLES: Fan, Heart

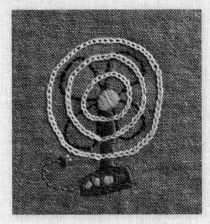

The chain stitch is a really fancy-looking stitch, but in fact, it's super simple. Bring the needle up from the wrong side of the fabric at A **(FIG. 26)**. Bring it down at B, as close to A as you can (or even back down through A), leaving a loop of thread on the top side of the fabric **(FIG. 27)**. Make sure not to pull the thread and the loop all the way through the fabric. Bring your needle back up inside the top point of the loop, at C **(FIG. 28)**. Pull the loop taut. Repeat those steps, with C becoming your new A **(FIG. 29)** and D becoming your new B **(FIG. 30)**.

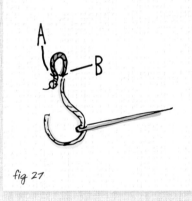

fig 26

fig 27

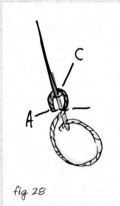

fig 28

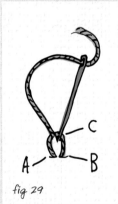

fig 29

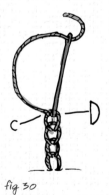

fig 30

SEED STITCH →

Use as a fun filling stitch to add texture and a subtle hint of color to a design area .

EXAMPLES: Can (directional stitches), Cactus (partly directional stitches), Hot dog (random direction stitches)

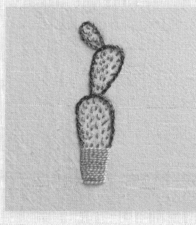

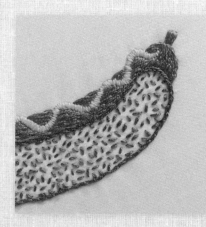

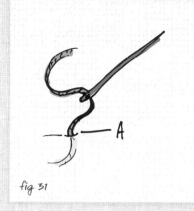

fig 31

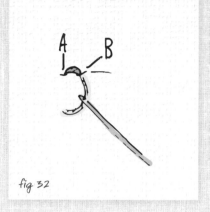

fig 32

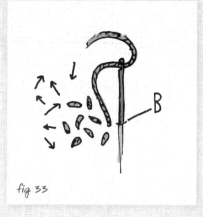

fig 33

The seed stitch is very useful if you don't have the time, patience, or quantity of thread to fill in an area with satin stitches or split stitches. Seed stitches can add a nice, even field of color and interesting texture. You can do them at random angles, or all in one direction, or mix the direction if there is more than one design element in the embroidery, to suggest different textures and create different effects. You can even use different thicknesses of threads in each design element.

Pull the needle up from the wrong side of the fabric at A **(FIG. 31)** and down at B to create a single stitch **(FIG. 32)**. Repeat at random directions **(FIG. 33)** or in the same direction. Work from one end of the area to be filled, to the opposite end, so as to not overlap your stitching.

Embroidery Woes

If you are new to embroidery, it might take you a while to figure out what stitches and colors you like best. I certainly find myself questioning my choices on a regular basis. Be confident in yourself; if you chose the colors or stitches in the first place, it was probably the right choice. But if you still find yourself unhappy with your work, there are ways to salvage it.

Covering stitches

If you've made stitches to embroider an outline on a design element and just aren't loving how it looks, whether it doesn't pop enough or the color just isn't right, you can cover it up. Use a closely spaced couching stitch (opposite page) and a new thread color to stitch over your previous stitches. Here's an example of how I did this with the bow embroidery.

Beefing up stitches

Sometimes you've done a really nice stitch to outline a design element, only to find that it "disappears" on the base fabric you've chosen. I did this with the stem of the flower shown here. A really easy fix is to add another row or two of the same stitch alongside your original stitches to thicken your outline. Easy peasy.

Ripping out stitches

This is the last resort. It might make you cry the first time you have to do it, especially if you've spent a good amount of time on the embroidery, but it's worth it in the end. If you are still working with the same thread or have just started a thread and want to change, use the eye end of your needle to pull out the thread from the sections or outlines you need to remove. If you've already finished the stitching, you may need to cut out your work with scissors. Use small sharp-pointed scissors or a seam ripper. Gently pull out what you can with your fingers and use tweezers for any fine threads that remain. If the color you're ripping out was one of the first you stitched and you've since stitched over the back of it, be extremely careful not to snag or stretch your other stitches. If you've torn out stitches and are still seeing needle holes, try turning your fabric over and running the back of your fingernail along the holes to smooth them out.

COUCHING STITCH ↘

Use this stitch to outline motifs, create curved and straight lines, and to add a decorative border to an embroidery.

EXAMPLES: Horseshoe, Tag (string)

I really like couching because it is an interesting and decorative way to lay down a long thread and tack it in place. It requires two threads, one thicker and one thinner, which can be the same or different colors, to add texture and interest. You can even lay down a group of threads and tack them in place the same way.

Start by pulling the needle with your first thread (the "laid" thread) up from the wrong side of the fabric at A and hold that thread down along the line of your motif **(FIG. 34)**. Pull up the needle with the second thread (the "couching" thread) at B and stitch down at C, on the opposite side of your laid thread, to secure the laid thread **(FIG. 35)** in place. At the end of the row, pull the ends of all threads to the wrong side and secure them.

You can make your couching stitches as close together as you like—very close **(FIG. 36)** or more widely spaced **(FIG. 37)**. But make sure not to space the couching stitches farther than ½ inch (1.3 cm) apart, or your laid thread may loosen and slip off the motif lines.

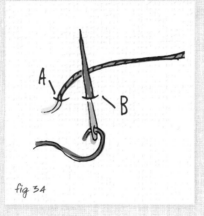

fig 34

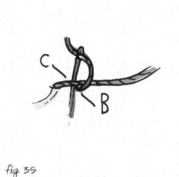

fig 35

fig 36

fig 37

Creative Ideas

CHOOSING COLOR

Choosing color can be a very personal matter. Some people are naturally confident in their color selections, but for those of us who sometimes struggle to settle on a main color, or to decide what accent colors to add, here are a few tips.

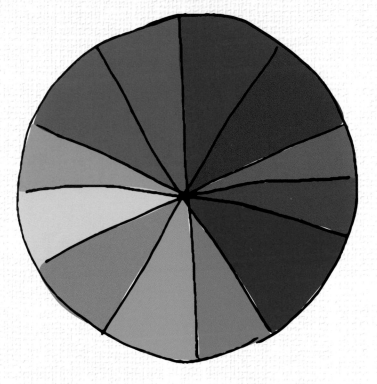

Use the color wheel

There are many ways to go about choosing colors, but the color wheel is the most common, easy-to-use tool. You can find a color wheel tool to help you make combinations at most craft, art supply, and stores where you find embroidery supplies. The most basic color wheel starts with the three primary colors—red, yellow, and blue. If you mix these colors in various combinations, you'll end up with a very complex wheel, including colors such as yellow-green, blue-green, blue-violet, and so on. Some basic ideas for selecting colors from the color wheel are shown here.

ANALOGOUS

COMPLEMENTARY

SPLIT COMPLEMENTARY

ANALOGOUS colors are three colors on the color wheel that touch each other. A fun example is red, pink, and violet.

COMPLEMENTARY (or direct complementary) colors are two colors that are exactly opposite each other on the color wheel. Expand on this palette by adding neighboring colors.

A **SPLIT COMPLEMENTARY** color scheme includes one color plus two colors that lie on each side of its complement on the color wheel. You split the complement into two adjacent colors, in other words. An example is blue plus red-orange and yellow-orange.

When you are working with split complementary combinations, you can take your favorite color as a starting point and work from there on the color wheel. If you love lime green (a yellow-green on the color wheel), you can add grass green (a green on the color wheel) and teal (a blue-green on the color wheel).

When choosing thread colors, always take into consideration the color of your background fabric.

When choosing thread colors, always take into consideration the color of your background fabric. A thread color can look immensely different on different background colors, so it's always important to keep that in mind when planning thread purchases. Even better, take a sample of the background fabric with you when you shop for thread.

Use color resources

Books, magazines, and the Internet are great sources for collecting color ideas. (Pinterest is a particularly wonderful source of color inspiration.) On the Internet, search for "color palette" or "color scheme." You're bound to come up with plenty of results, especially with the explosion of online color resources in recent years. Take a look at any images you like on the Internet or pull one of your favorite photos from a magazine or your own stash of inspirational imagery. From the photos, try to pick out the three main colors

you see, as well as two or three secondary accent colors you like, to create your palette. Match the main colors you have picked to the larger areas of your embroidery, saving the accompanying colors for smaller details.

Plot out your embroidery colors

Because the motifs included in this book are black-and-white outline drawings, you can work with them as you would with designs in a coloring book. Once you have decided on your palette, trace or make an extra copy of your chosen motif. Use colored pencils, paint, or markers to color in the motif as you imagine it. Color just the outlines if you plan on embroidering only those. If you're planning on using a satin stitch, split stitch, or other stitch to completely fill in an area, color in that area. This is a great way to preplan your embroidery, and it will help keep you on track as you are working.

From the photos, try to pick out the three main colors you see, as well as two or three secondary accent colors you like, to create your palette.

where to start

Embroidery is fun, because with the same set of simple stitches, a first timer, as well as a seasoned veteran, can create her or his own interpretation of the same design. The only difference is experience. When I look back at my first embroideries—just like my first drawings—they seem a bit simple, maybe even juvenile, but still beautiful. With practice, everything changes and improves. I really haven't learned too many new stitches; I like to stick to the basics. But the ones I do use, I've gotten much better at.

If you're a beginner, I suggest that you try the simpler, smaller motifs in this book first. It's good to get a feel for the stitches and how you can manipulate them before you jump into the larger-scale motifs. Work your way up to larger projects when you're feeling more confident about your stitching abilities. You'll find yourself breezing through projects in no time at all.

CREATIVE USES FOR FINISHED EMBROIDERIES

How often do you actually plan out what you will do with your finished embroidery project before you choose your design and start stitching? I almost never do. I just like to pick up fabric and thread and get going, and that's a wonderful way to work—for me anyway. But there is a great alternative—planning! Planning what to do with your embroidery before you create it is the best way to make the most of your time. Following are some great uses for particular types of embroideries you'll find in this book.

SMALL MOTIFS

Everyone loves those little chest-pocket motifs on polo shirts, right? At least, I do. But I would much rather have my own design there. The tiny, penny-sized motifs in this book were meant for polo shirts, as well as for make-believe scout badges, zipper pulls, and more small spots. Embroider the teeny-tiny dinosaur (page 120) on a child's T-shirt or the bitsy wrapped candy (page 55) on a gift tag.

For a really special project, make use of tiny motifs to produce a sweet embroidered fabric that you can use for clothing or accessories. On a full piece of fabric, stitch evenly spaced small embroideries to create an allover design. You can repeat the same design or mix up different ones.

Some fun ideas for using small motifs.

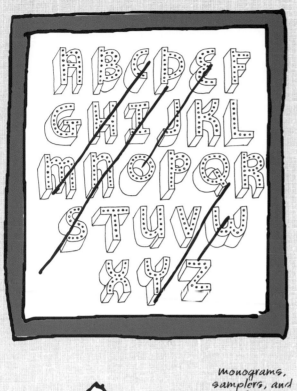

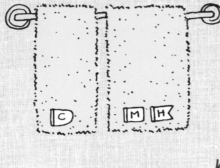

Create an embroidered clothing label

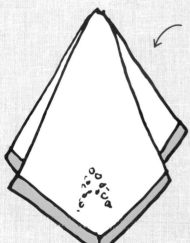

monograms, samplers, and initials for clothing and towels are great uses for embroidered alphabet letters.

ALPHABETS

The alphabets in this book (page 140) are really wonderful for all kinds of projects. The letters can be used individually or in a trio, as a monogram. This is a great way to personalize any item, from a backpack to a handkerchief to a Dopp kit. Monogrammed napkins make a really wonderful hostess gift.

Another great idea is to use embroidered initials as a clothing label. Create your embroidered letter on a small piece of fabric or ribbon and neatly hem the edges. Handsew it on the nape of a neckline or back of a handmade or store-bought piece of clothing to add a sweet handmade touch to clothes.

You can also use one of the full alphabets to stitch a traditional sampler. Trace the full alphabet onto a piece of fabric with at least 3 inches (7.6 cm) of space on each side of the motifs. Create your embroidery, press, and frame it. This makes great wall art for a baby's room.

BORDERS

The border designs in this book are very special to me. I love repeat patterns, and they comprise most of the design work I do on a day-to-day basis. I knew I had to include repeat patterns in this book!

These borders are extremely useful and can be applied to a number of projects. You can use them to add a special handstitched touch to any handmade accessory—a clutch purse or headband, for example. Pillowcases and kitchen towels are great canvases for your borders as well.

Add a special touch with borders on clutches and pillowcases.

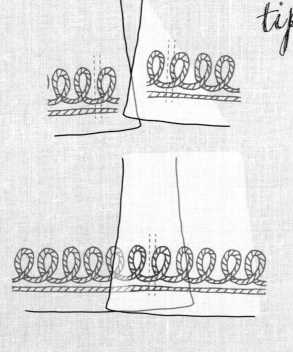

tip

The border motifs can be repeated to fill whatever space you would like. You will just need to set up the repeats when you are transferring or tracing the design onto your fabric. Once you have transferred the first length, simply match up and overlap the design elements at either end, from the left red dotted line to the right red dotted line. Keep repeating this process until you have covered your desired length of fabric.

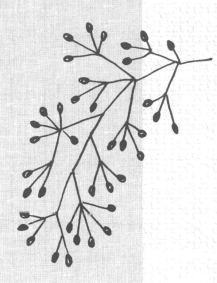

Resizing Embroideries

The motifs in this book should generally be used at no smaller than the sizes they are printed here. If you're a practiced stitcher, you could try making some of them smaller, but it can be tough to get in all of the details needed at a reduced size.

However, the motifs in this book can be easily scaled up in size for use in different situations and projects. If you are planning on enlarging a motif, there are some things you might want to keep in mind.

Types of stitches for enlarged motifs. It will be difficult to execute satin stitch and French knots at a very large scale. Better choices for larger embroideries are the backstitch or straight stitch. Also, a tight chain stitch can create the illusion of a nice, thick outline, so that is a great option for large-scale embroideries.

Thread choice. If you are creating an embroidery that is 10 inches (25.5 cm) or larger and will be on a heavy or textured material—say for a blanket, throw pillow, or cool denim jacket—you will need a relatively thick thread so that the image will be visible. I tend to use yarn or all six strands of embroidery floss in cases like these. Make sure the yarn is not loosely spun, or the twist will separate in mid-stitch. Remember to size up your needle as you size up your thread. Along with increasing the size of those two supplies, you'll need to consider the fabric you are using as well. The results will look much better if you choose a fabric that can accommodate the size of your needle and thread, so look for a looser weave, or heavier fabric, rather than something light and thin, like quilting cotton, which will show large holes. If the weave is loose enough that you feel your embroidery might show through to the back, add interfacing to the back that is as close to the same color of your fabric as possible.

How to resize motifs

A copy machine is a great tool for resizing an embroidery design. Most copiers have easy-to-use "scale up" and "scale down" buttons. Copy-service stores are nearly everywhere. Most public libraries allow low-cost copy machine use, and your librarian would probably love to help you if you have trouble with the machine. (If you have a grumpy librarian, I apologize for this tip!)

Of course, if you use the patterns from the CD at the back of this book, you can easily resize them on your computer!

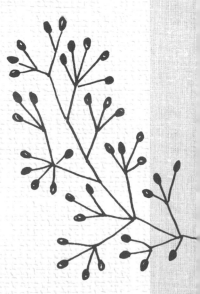

Frame designs add personal touches to items, like this personalized quilt label.

FRAMES

The frame designs I've created for this book (pages 128–131) have a great variety of end uses. I first imagined these as quilt labels. Anyone who has put in all the work it takes to make a quilt will agree that the finished product deserves a label that is just as beautiful. Use your own handwriting to fill in details. You can stitch over your writing with a thin thread or keep it simple and write in the details in permanent ink.

The frames are also a great way to personalize items. Use a frame motif to create a stitched book cover, a patch for a homemade present, or gift tag, and use your own handwriting to write a person's name or anything else you want inside the frame, either with thread or with permanent ink.

OTHER USES FOR EMBROIDERIES

CREATE A BROOCH OR PIN by adding a fabric backing and a bar pin.

PLAN AN EMBROIDERED ACCENT for a sewing project. When cutting out a pattern piece for a bag, for example, trace your chosen motif onto the bag fabric piece, making sure to allow room for your seams. Sew together your professional-looking project!

MAKE A COOL PATCH for clothing by hemming and stitching your finished embroidery onto a jacket, shirt, or pants pocket.

Embroider on fabric before cutting it out to make a one-of-a-kind sewing project.

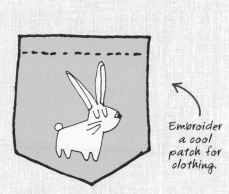

Embroider a cool patch for clothing.

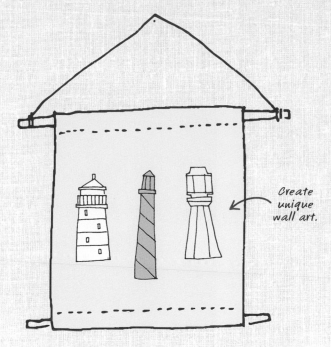

Create unique wall art.

MAKE A SAMPLER by choosing a series of motifs to your liking, perhaps sticking to a theme. Embroider in the center of a large piece of fabric, making sure to leave 3 inches (7.6 cm) on each side for framing. Hang on your wall or give as a wonderful handmade gift.

make a holiday ornament featuring an embroidery.

CREATE A HOLIDAY ORNAMENT by placing your embroidery right sides together with a piece of backing fabric and stitching around the edges, leaving an opening for stuffing. Stuff with pinches of cotton or polyester batting, stitch the opening closed, add a string or piece of pearl cotton at the top—and hang!

FRAME AN EMBROIDERY to use as a small piece of wall art. Use a traditional frame or sew a hanging sleeve on the back of the fabric at the top edge and slide a dowel through it to make a banner.

Embroider a collar before sewing a garment.

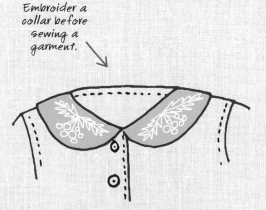

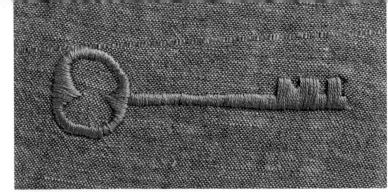

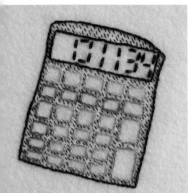
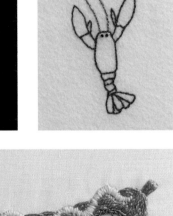

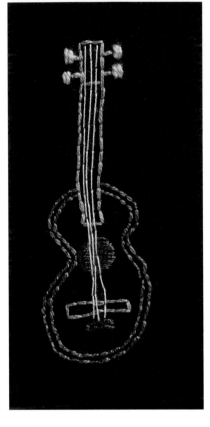

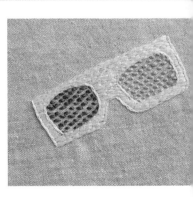

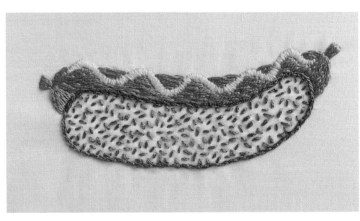

The Patterns

I love creating images of all aspects of life. In the following pages, you'll find 750+ motifs depicting some of my favorite things. They're organized according to themes, such as garden, kitchen, crafts, food, and more. I've also included motifs for popular and useful themes such as School Days and The Great Outdoors. Motifs range from teeny tiny to large and include something to appeal to everyone's taste! In addition, two special sections—Frames & Borders and Alphabets—offer these useful designs in a great variety of style options.

NOTE: All the patterns printed in this section also appear on the CD at the back of this book. For instructions on how to use the CD, see page 151.

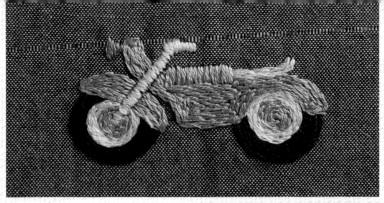

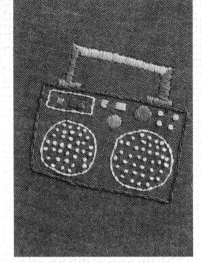

Made in
the USA

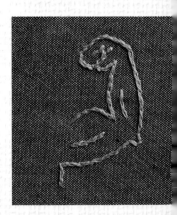

hot rod

motorcycle

vintage car

food truck

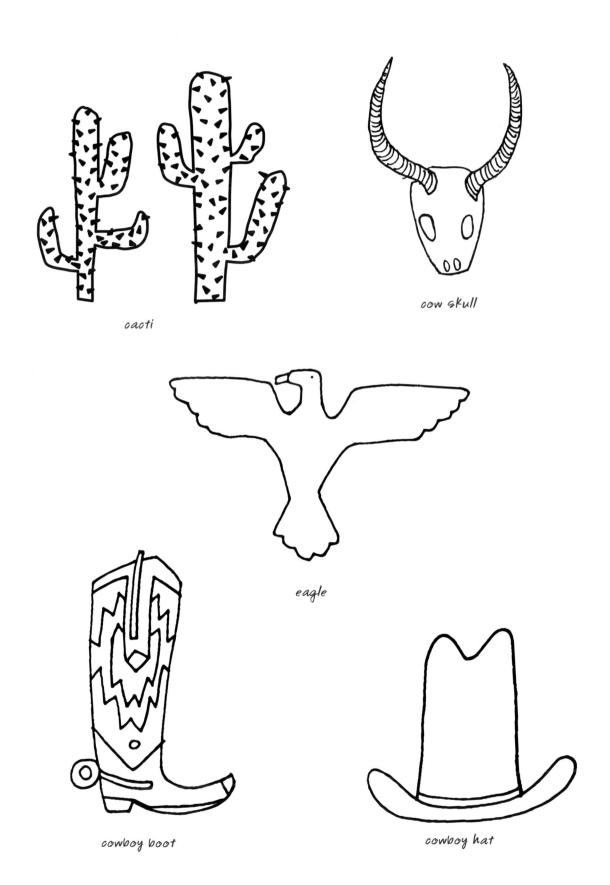

cacti

cow skull

eagle

cowboy boot

cowboy hat

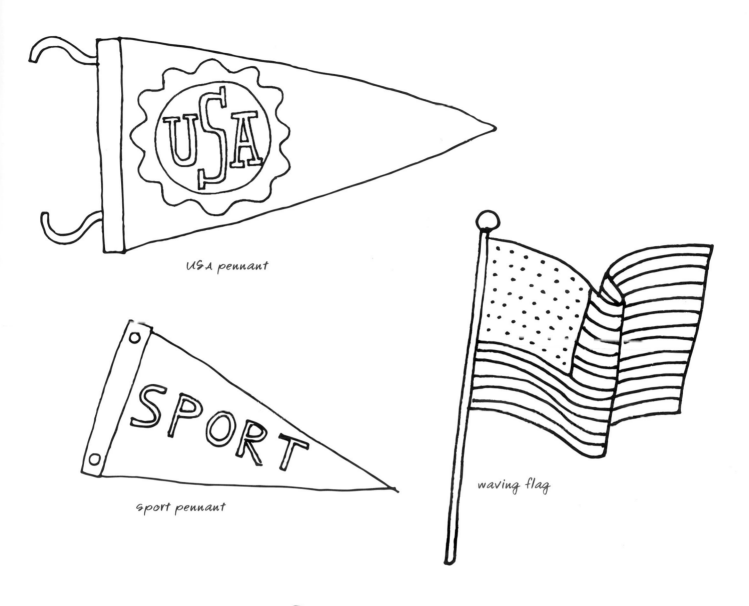

USA pennant

sport pennant

waving flag

firefighter badge

strong arm

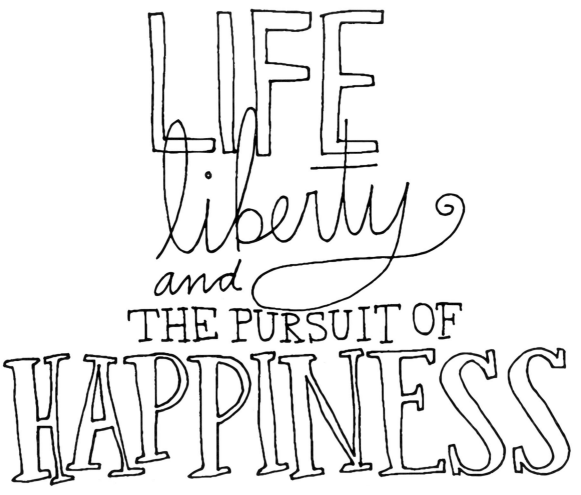

life, liberty, happiness lettering

5-cent flower stamp

5-cent stamp

coin

1-cent bird stamp

10-cent stamp

dollar bill

boom box

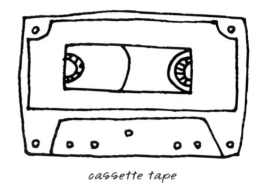

cassette tape

beer

bingo card

dominos

scene clapper

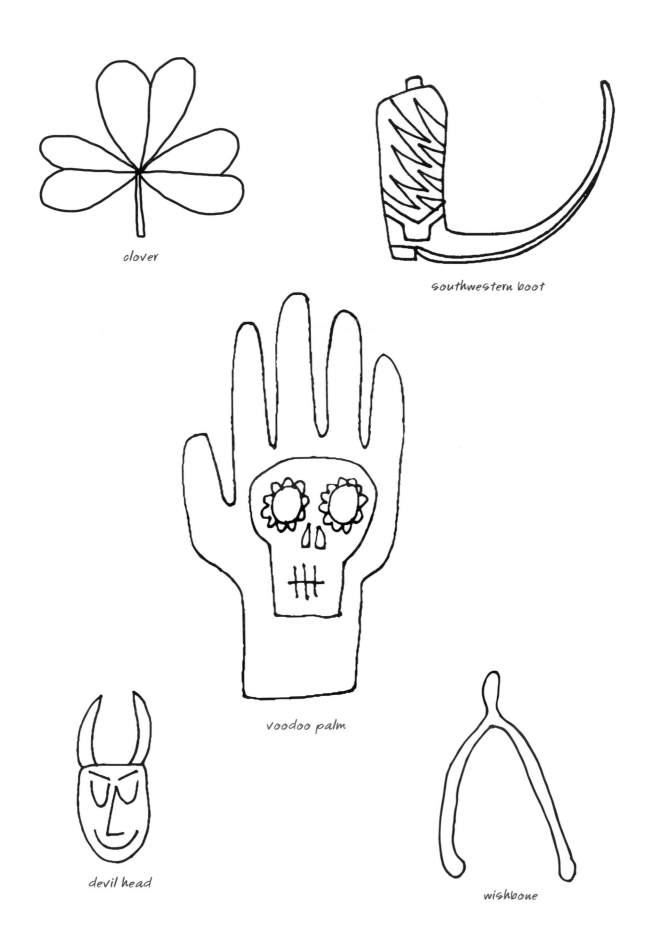

clover

southwestern boot

voodoo palm

devil head

wishbone

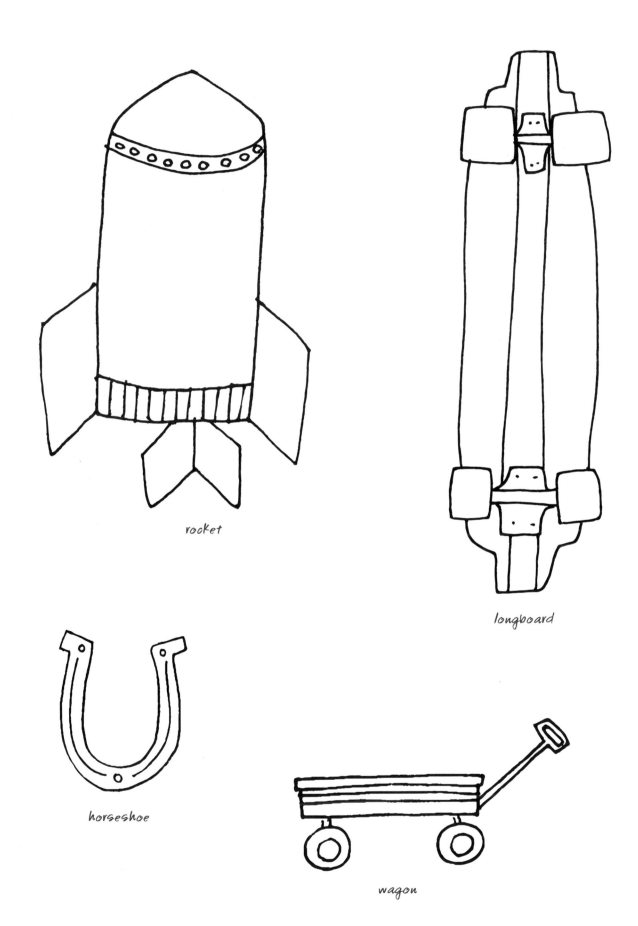

rocket

longboard

horseshoe

wagon

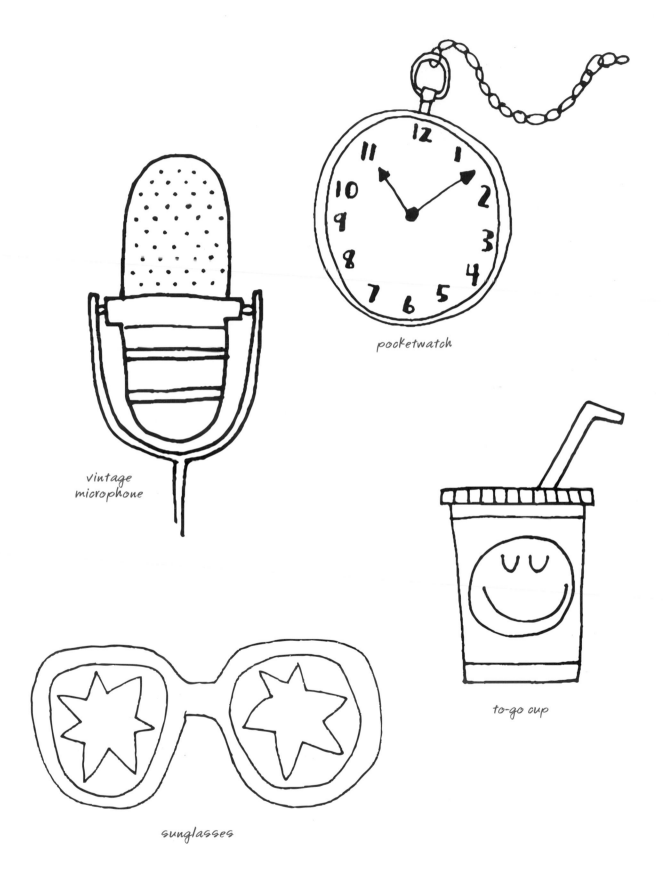

pocketwatch

vintage
microphone

to-go cup

sunglasses

Food

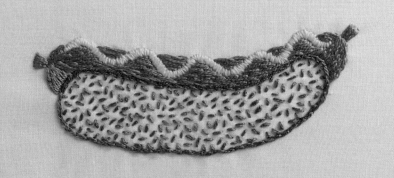

cherries

peppers

corn

lemon

melon

pineapple

pear

peach

pizza
slice

ice cream
cone

soft-serve cone

frosted donut

hamburger

fruit on scale

mini orange

mini french fries

mini burger

mini drink

mini hot dog

mini watermelon

lollipop

candy

JELLY BEANS

jelly beans

tea bag

TEA

breath mint

salmon nigiri

california roll

crab nigiri

shrimp nigiri

salmon roll

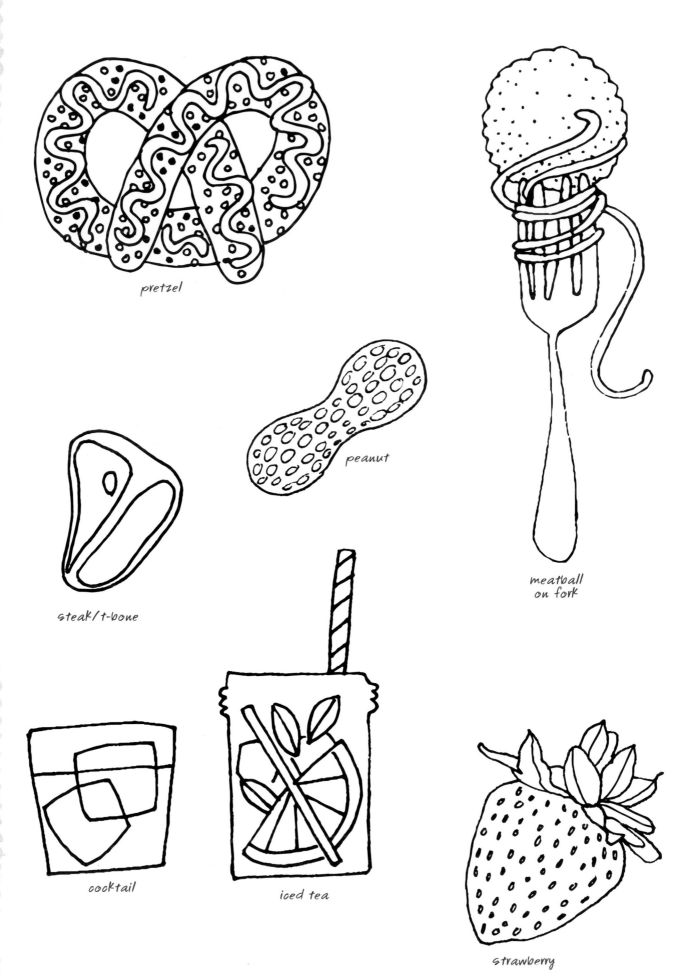

pretzel

peanut

meatball
on fork

steak/t-bone

cocktail

iced tea

strawberry

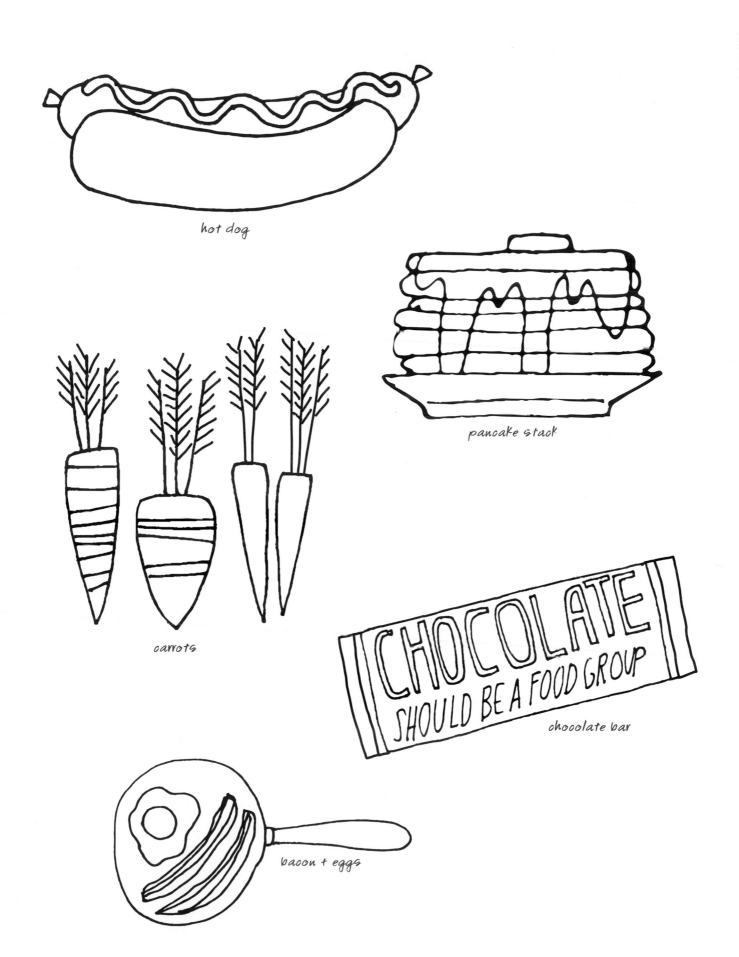

hot dog

pancake stack

carrots

CHOCOLATE SHOULD BE A FOOD GROUP

chocolate bar

bacon + eggs

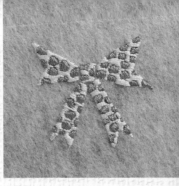

Craft Room

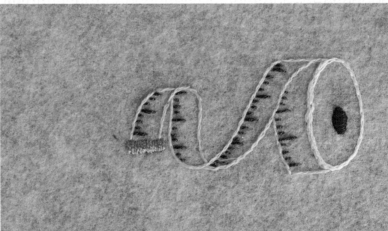

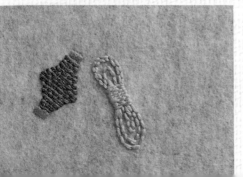

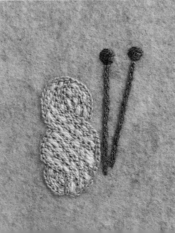

Learn to

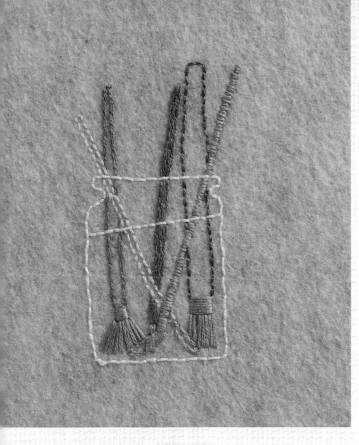

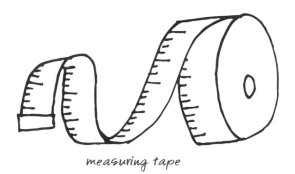

measuring tape

buttons

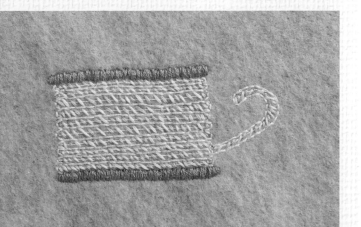

mini
pincushion

mini
scissors

mini
sewing machine

patterns

dress

iron

inkwell + dropper

jar of beads

hole punch

speckled
bow tie

polka-dot
bow

bow

bear claw

small bow

log cabin

flying geese

quilt block

star quilt block

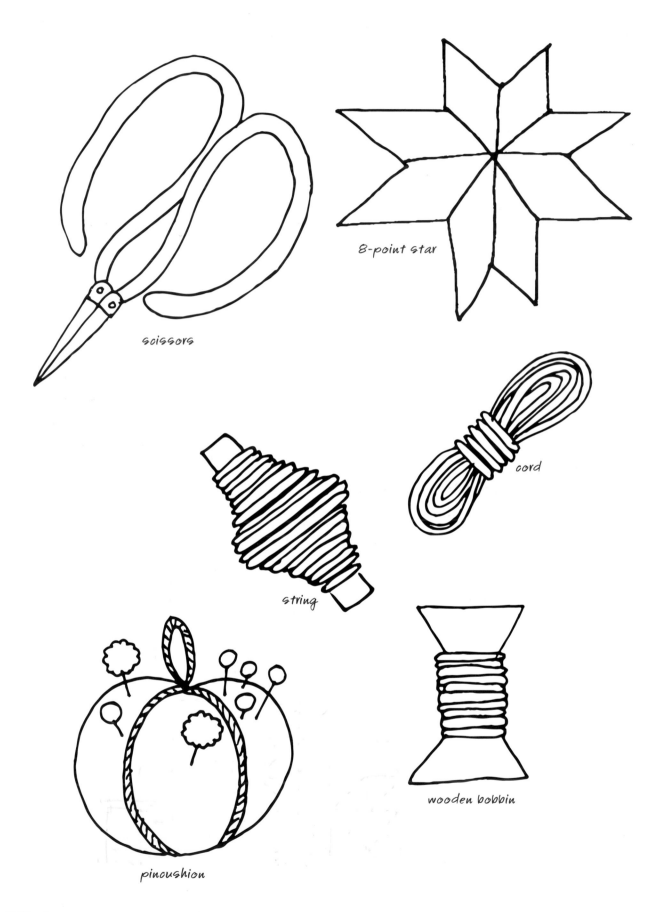

scissors

8-point star

string

cord

pincushion

wooden bobbin

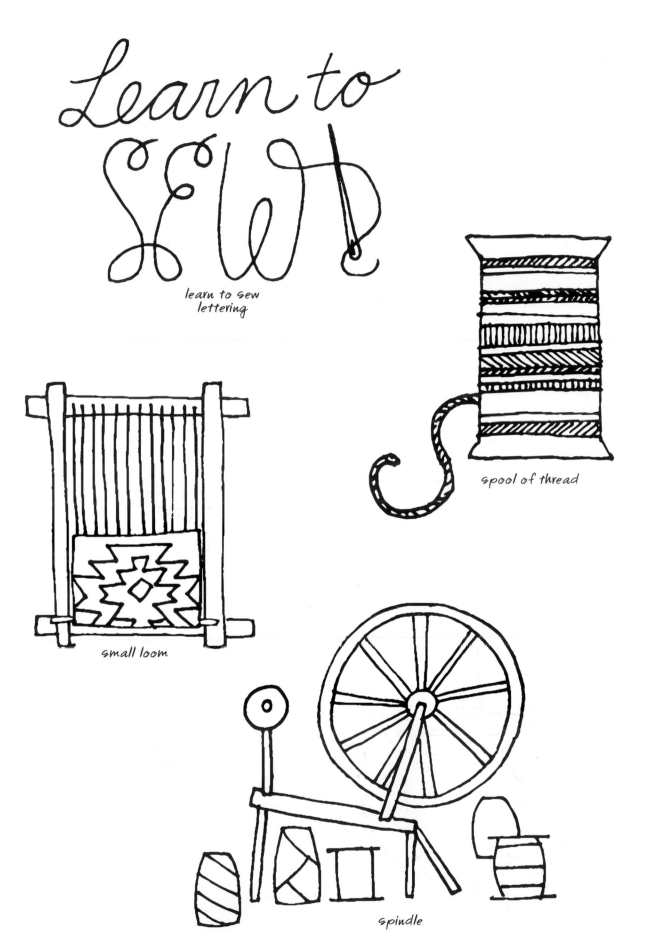

Learn to SEW

learn to sew
lettering

spool of thread

small loom

spindle

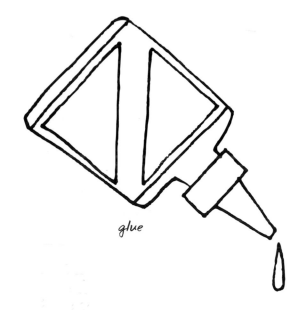

glue

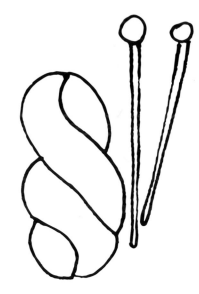

knitting needles
+ skein

vintage sewing machine

straight needles

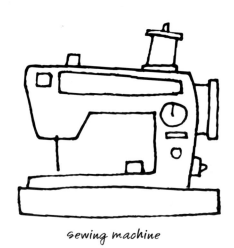

sewing machine

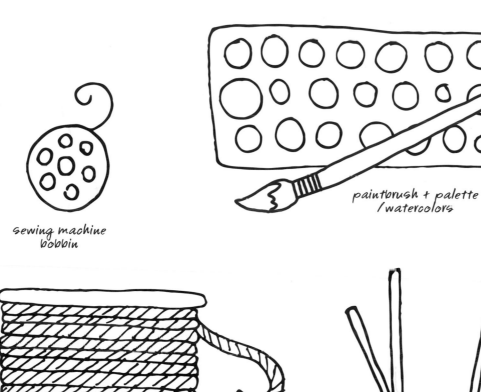

sewing machine
bobbin

paintbrush + palette
/watercolors

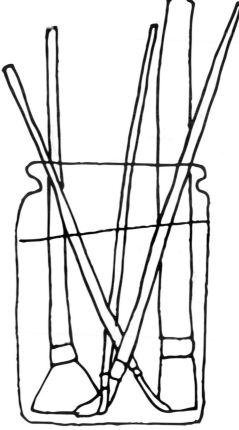

baker's twine

embellishments

jar of paintbrushes

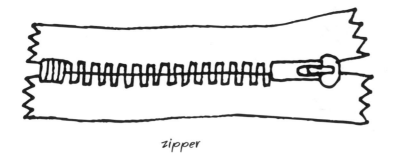

zipper

Tools of the Trade

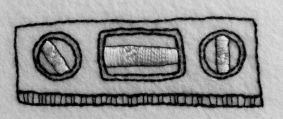

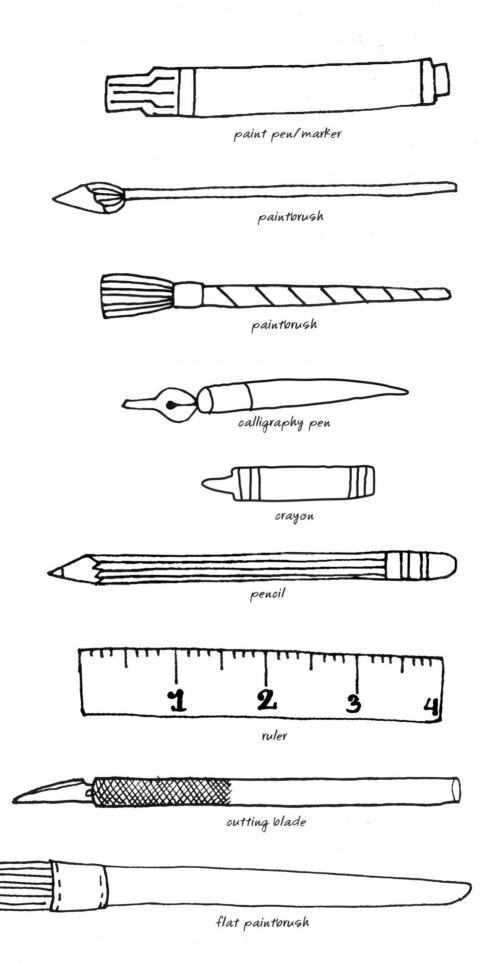

paint pen/marker

paintbrush

paintbrush

calligraphy pen

crayon

pencil

ruler

cutting blade

flat paintbrush

oil can

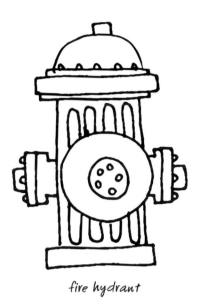

fire hydrant

calculator

spray paint

clipboard

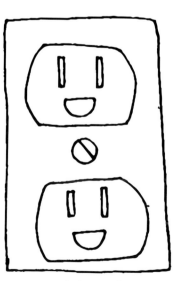

light socket

chainsaw

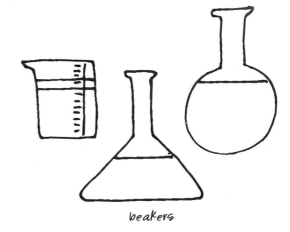

beakers

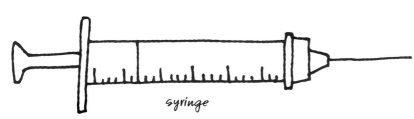

woodworking saw

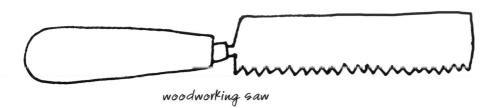

syringe

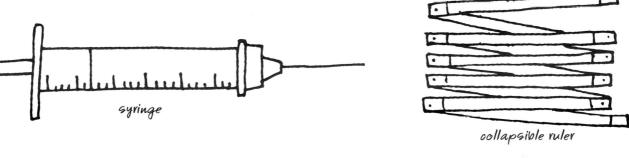

collapsible ruler

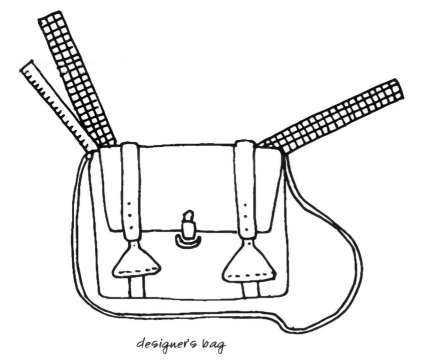

designer's bag

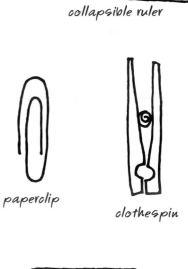

paperclip   clothespin

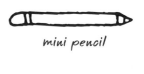

mini pencil

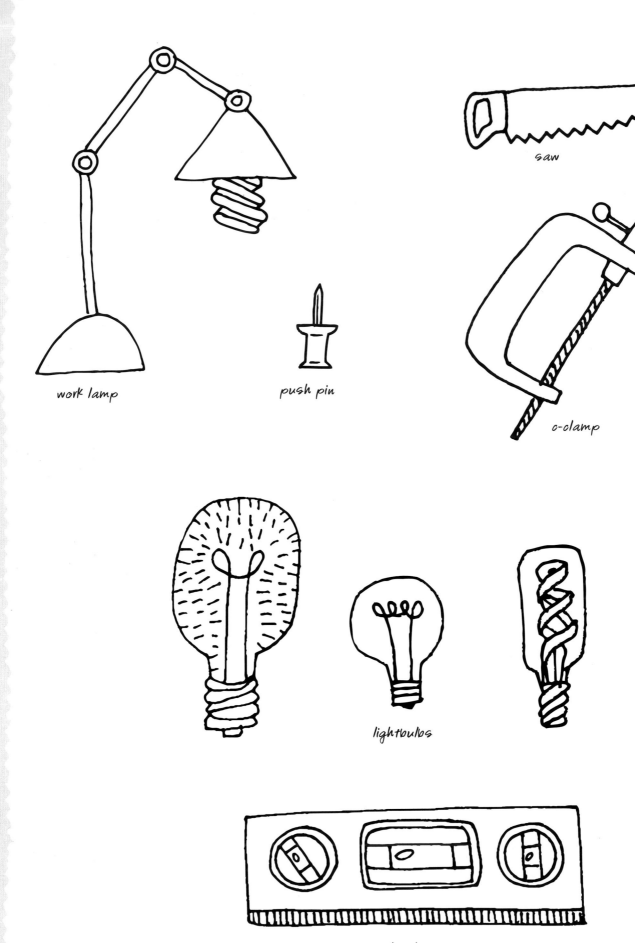

work lamp

push pin

saw

c-clamp

lightbulbs

level

screwdriver

nail

bolt

screw

nut

envelope

inkwell

wide paintbrush

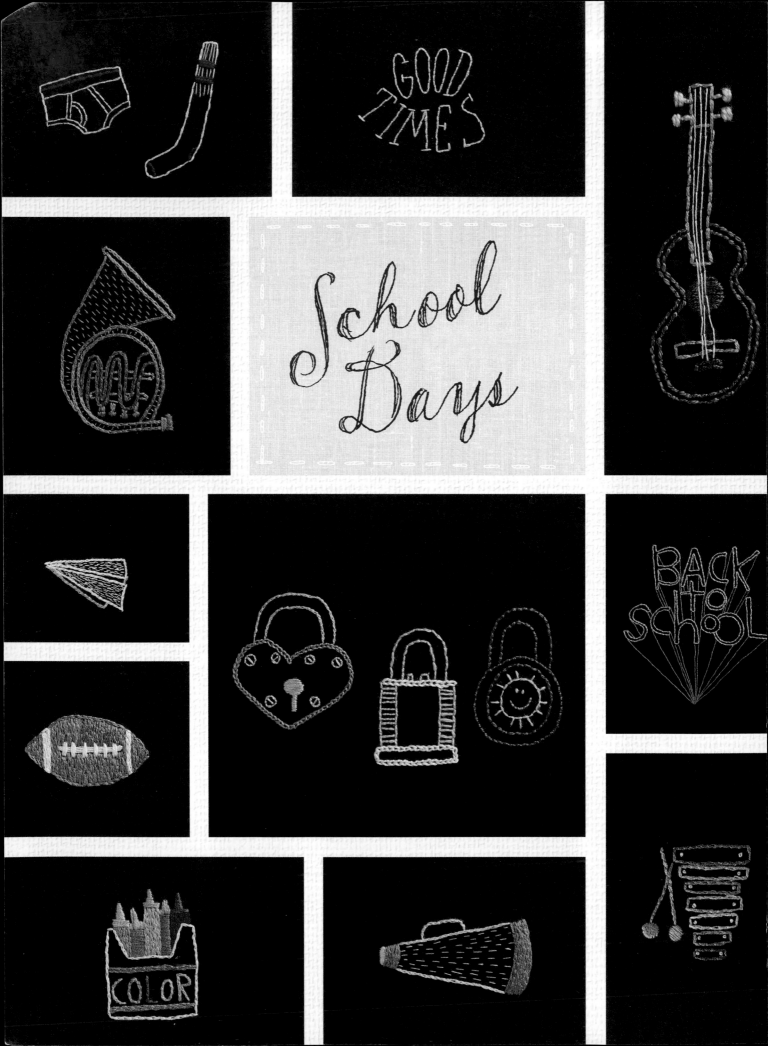

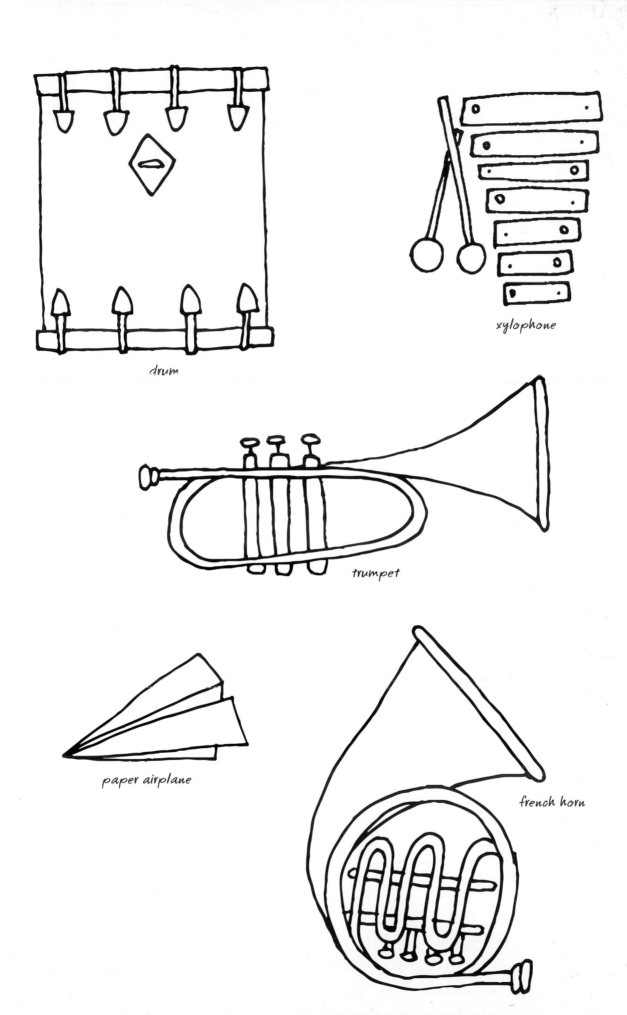

drum

xylophone

trumpet

paper airplane

french horn

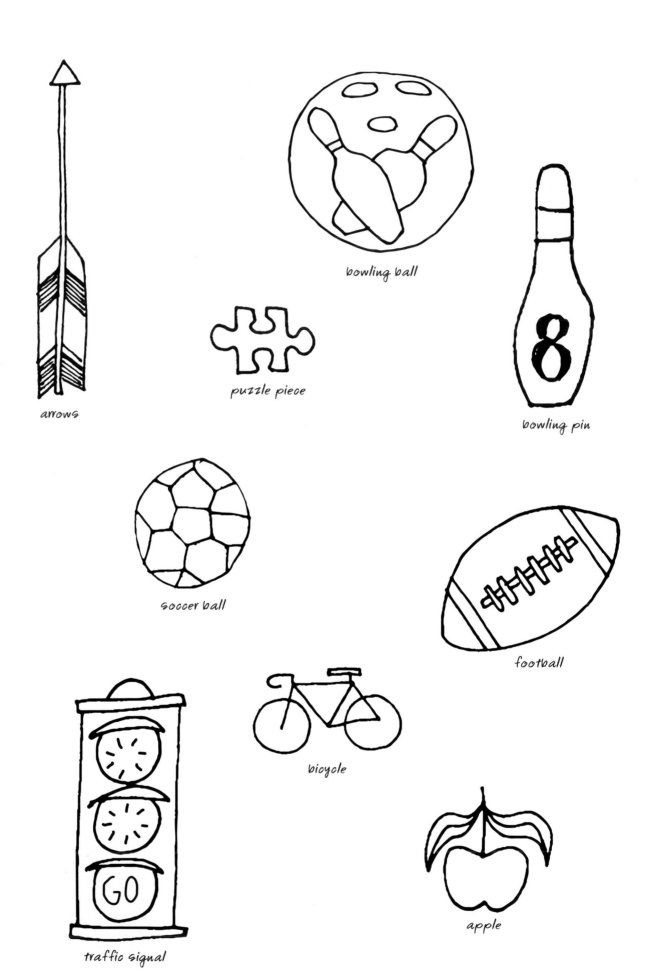

bowling ball

puzzle piece

arrows

bowling pin

soccer ball

football

bicycle

traffic signal

apple

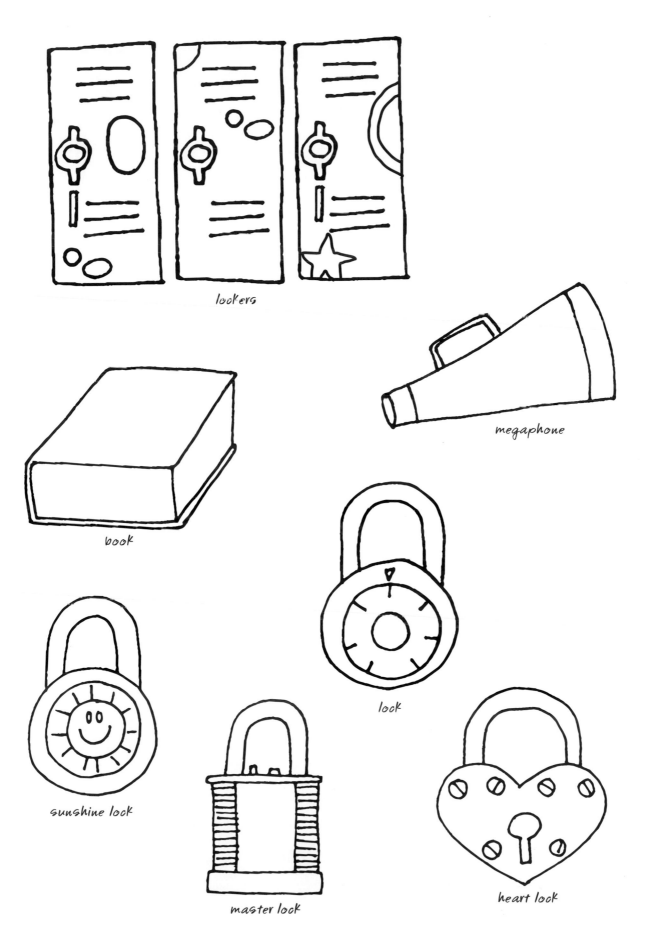

lockers

megaphone

book

lock

sunshine lock

master lock

heart lock

gym sock

banjo

guitar

mini tennis ball

mini baseball

mini football

mini notebook

mini apple

mini basketball

mini soccer ball

mini volleyball

globe

coach's whistle

stack of books

back to school
lettering

box of crayons

ballet shoes

good times
lettering

play lettering

chess piece/knight

chess piece/rook

chess piece/pawn

school bus

tightie whities

sports jersey

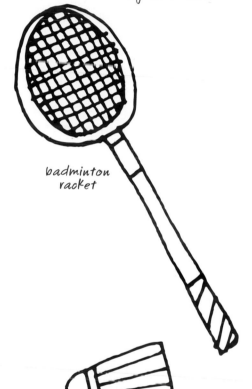

badminton
racket

badminton
shuttlecock

happy face

trophy

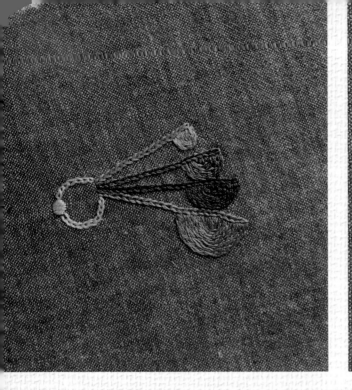

In the Kitchen

when life gives you LEMONS make lemonade

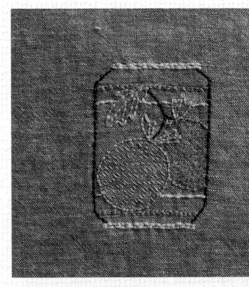

mouse in a teacup

mouse + cheese

floral teapot

mouse + mug

lemons in oil

teapot

electric mixer

thermos + mug

coffee kettle

toaster

when life gives you lemons make lemonade

lemons + lemonade lettering

milk bucket

espresso pot

salt + pepper shakers

vintage refrigerator

fork + happy spoon

chicken timer

mug

mini bottle

cleaver

knife

utensils

collander

milk carton

measuring pot

batter + spoon

measuring spoons

canned fruit

jam jar

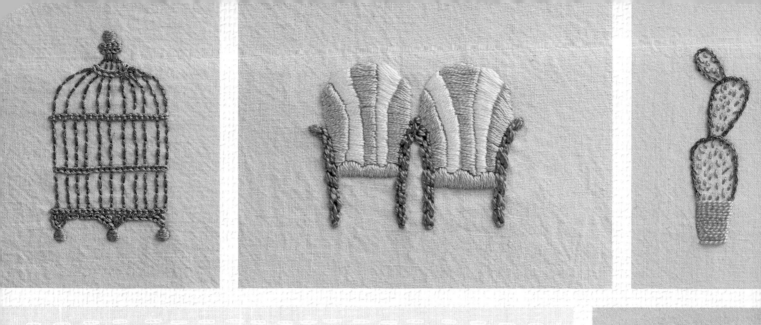

In the Garden

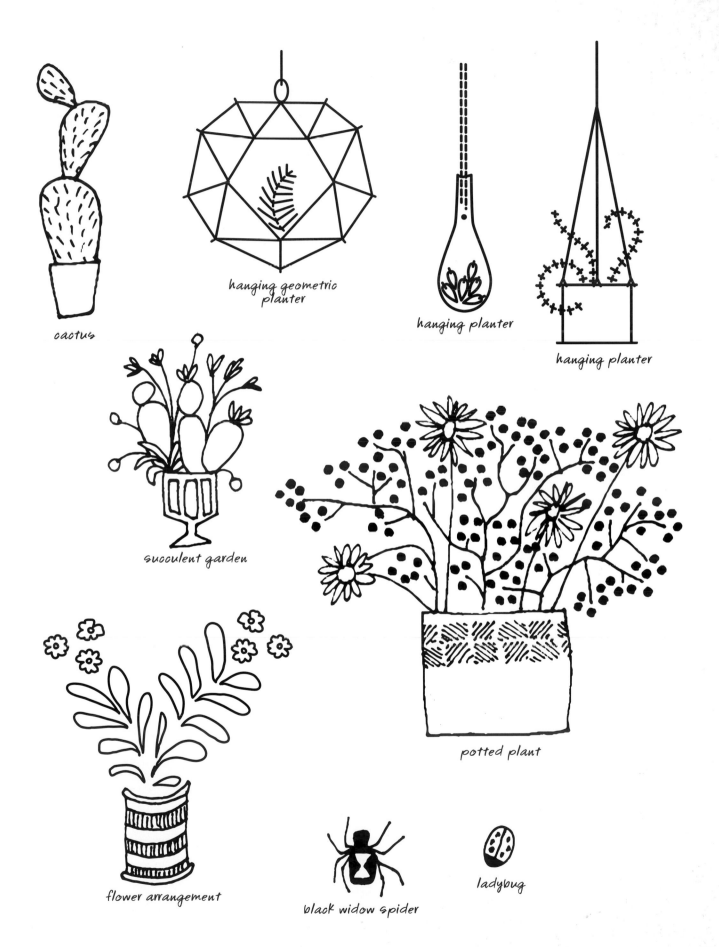

cactus

hanging geometric planter

hanging planter

hanging planter

succulent garden

potted plant

flower arrangement

black widow spider

ladybug

birdbath

lemon tree

leaping rabbit

watering can

artichokes

birdhouse

swan

succulent garden

yard flamingo

garden gnome

vegetable basket

outdoor loveseat

birdcage

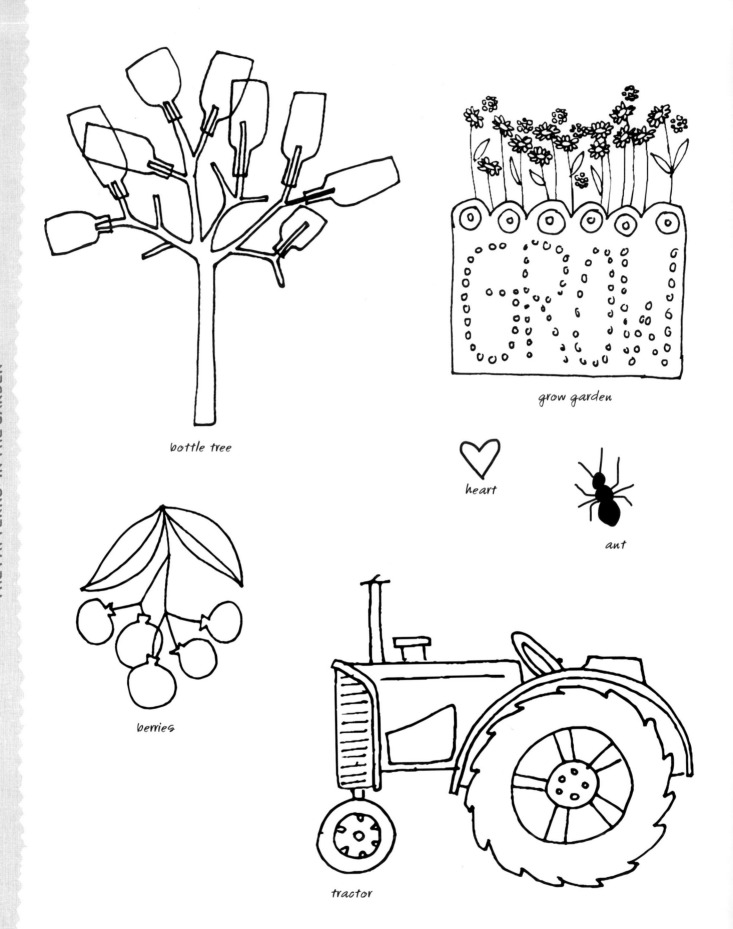

bottle tree

grow garden

heart

ant

berries

tractor

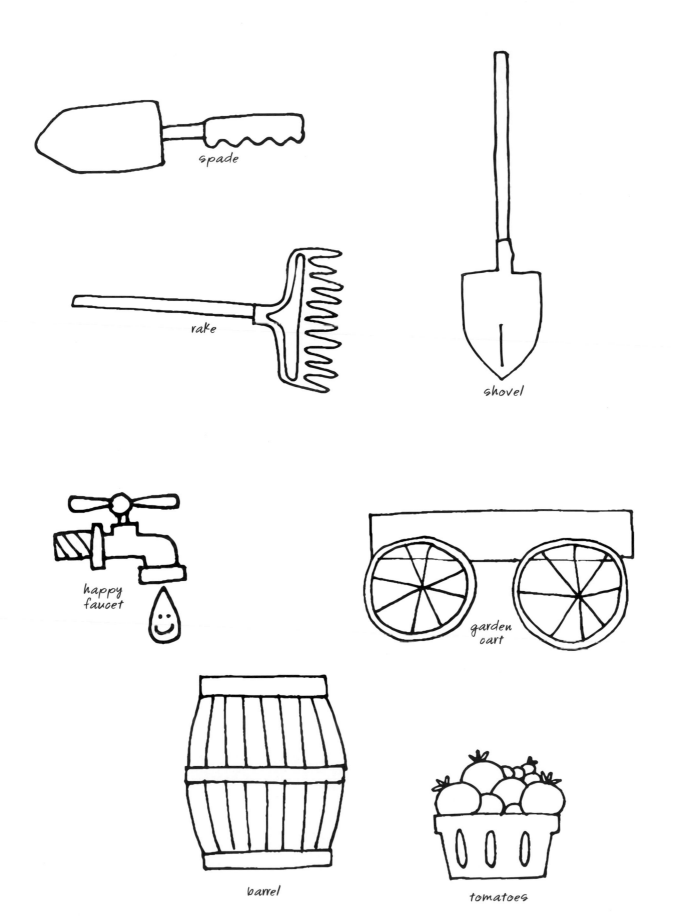

spade

rake

shovel

happy
faucet

garden
cart

barrel

tomatoes

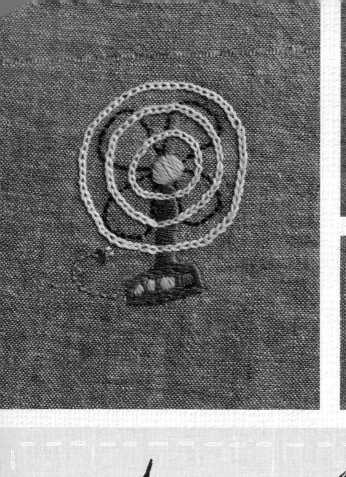
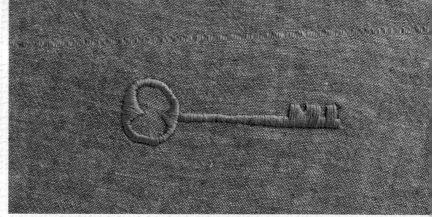

Around
the House

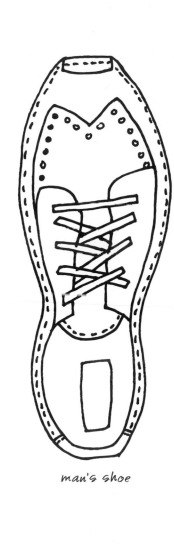

man's shoe

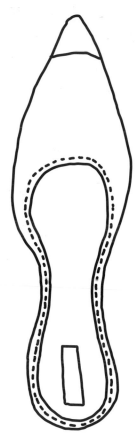

lady's shoe

plain sweater

fancy sweater

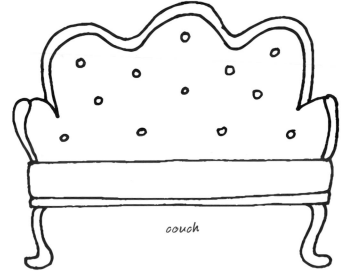

couch

alarm clock

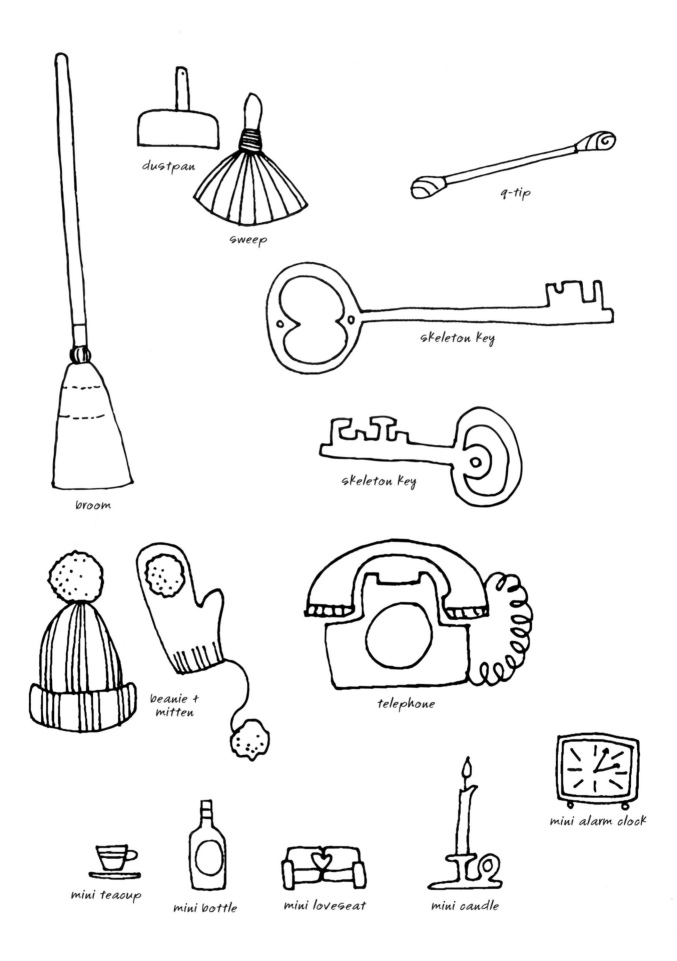

dustpan

sweep

q-tip

skeleton key

skeleton key

broom

beanie +
mitten

telephone

mini alarm clock

mini teacup

mini bottle

mini loveseat

mini candle

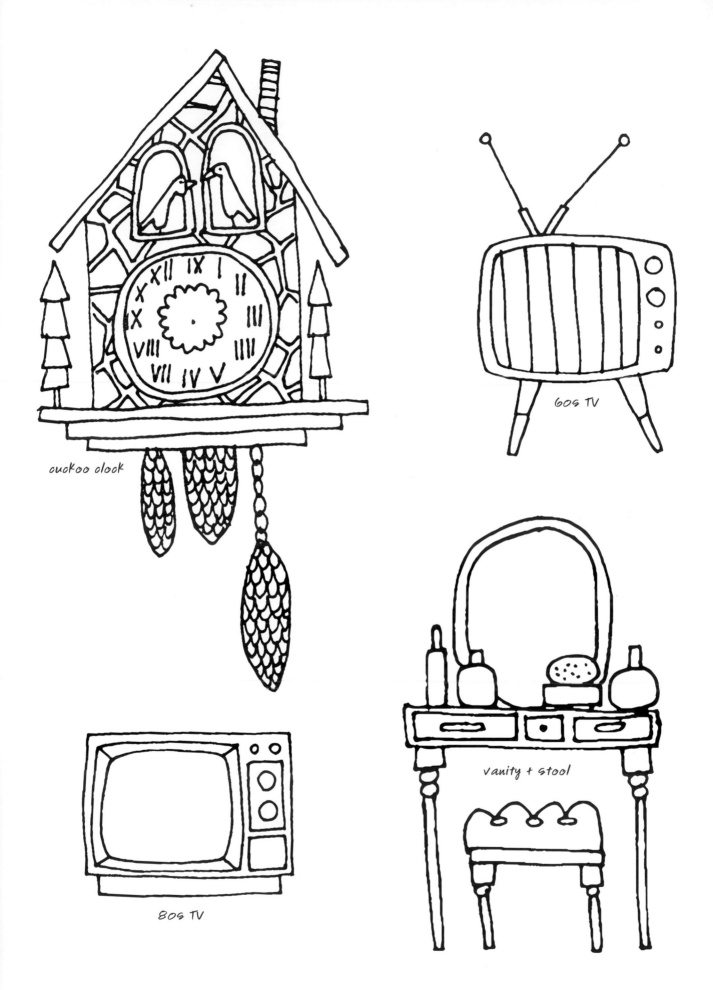

cuckoo clock

60s TV

80s TV

vanity + stool

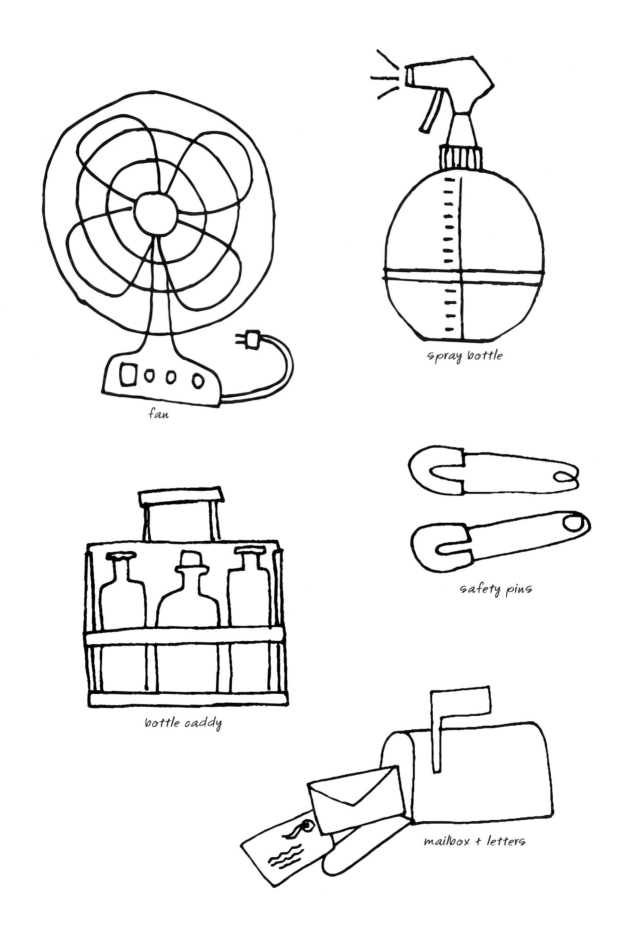

fan

spray bottle

safety pins

bottle caddy

mailbox + letters

front door

front door

front door

Fun!

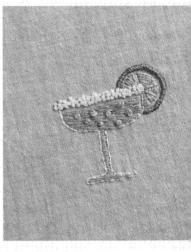

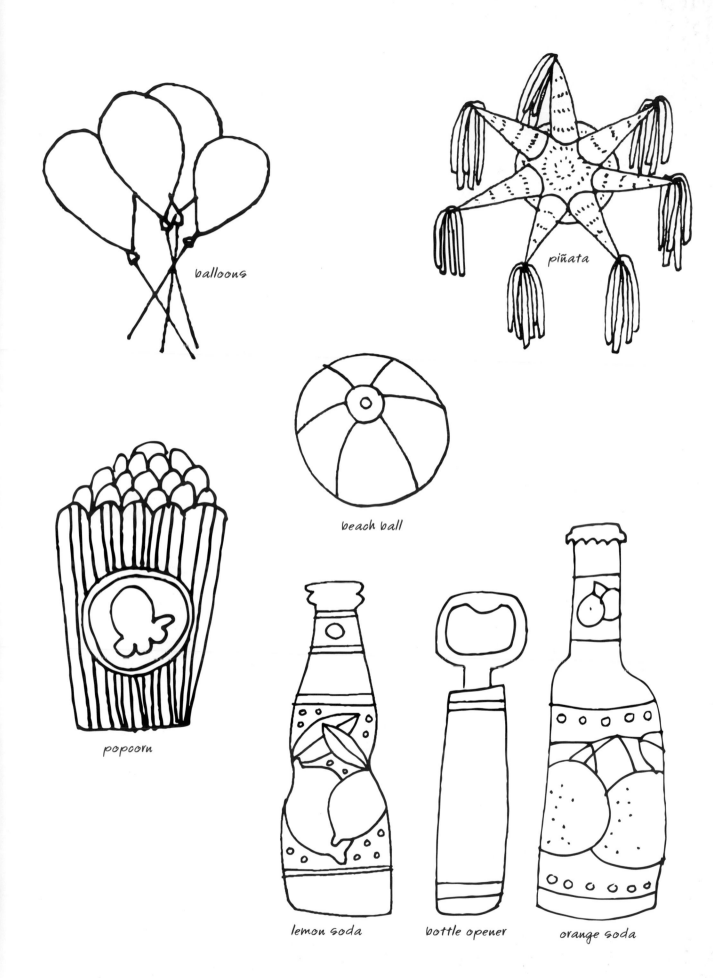

balloons

piñata

beach ball

popcorn

lemon soda

bottle opener

orange soda

disco ball

heart

star

olive +
toothpick

champagne
glasses

wrapped
present

martini

microphone

deck of
cards

dice

bottle

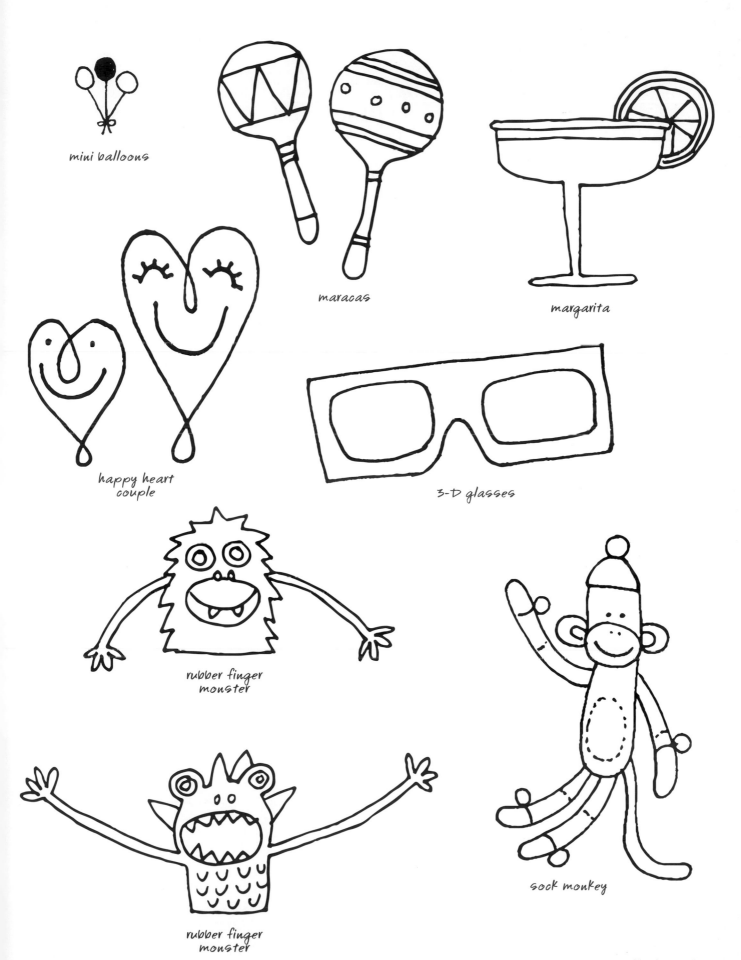

mini balloons

maracas

margarita

happy heart couple

3-D glasses

rubber finger monster

sock monkey

rubber finger monster

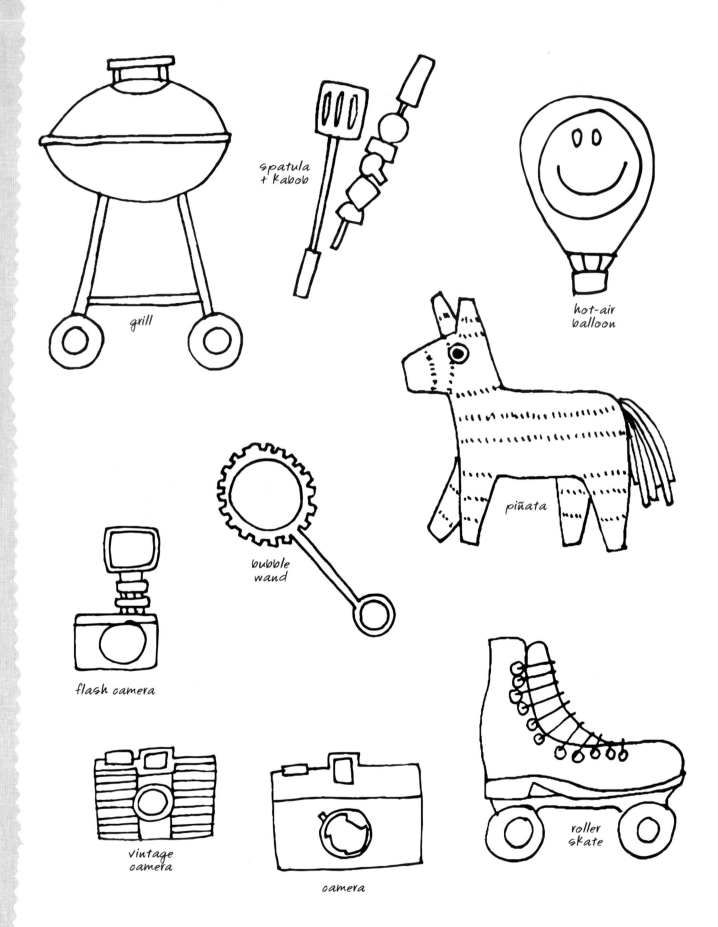

spatula + kabob

hot-air balloon

grill

piñata

bubble wand

flash camera

vintage camera

camera

roller skate

striped party hat

chevron party hat

heart + sword

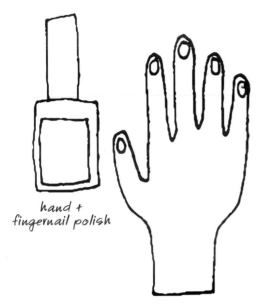

hand +
fingernail polish

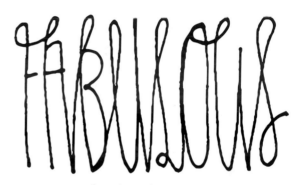

eyelashes

FABULOUS

fabulous lettering

crown

crown

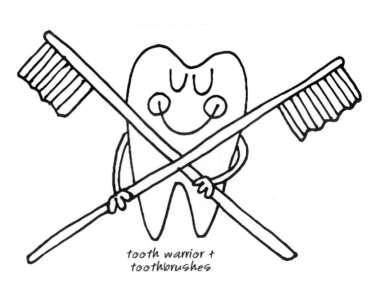

tooth warrior +
toothbrushes

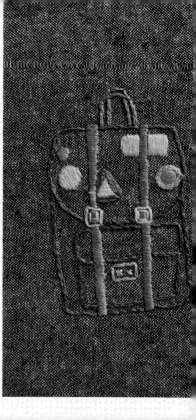

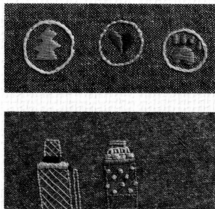

the Great Outdoors

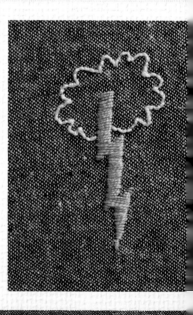

flies

army knife

lantern

camping knife

backpack

binoculars

boot

squirrel + acorn

fishing lure

overlander

first-aid badge

fishing lure

kombi + canoe

fishing lure

camper trailer

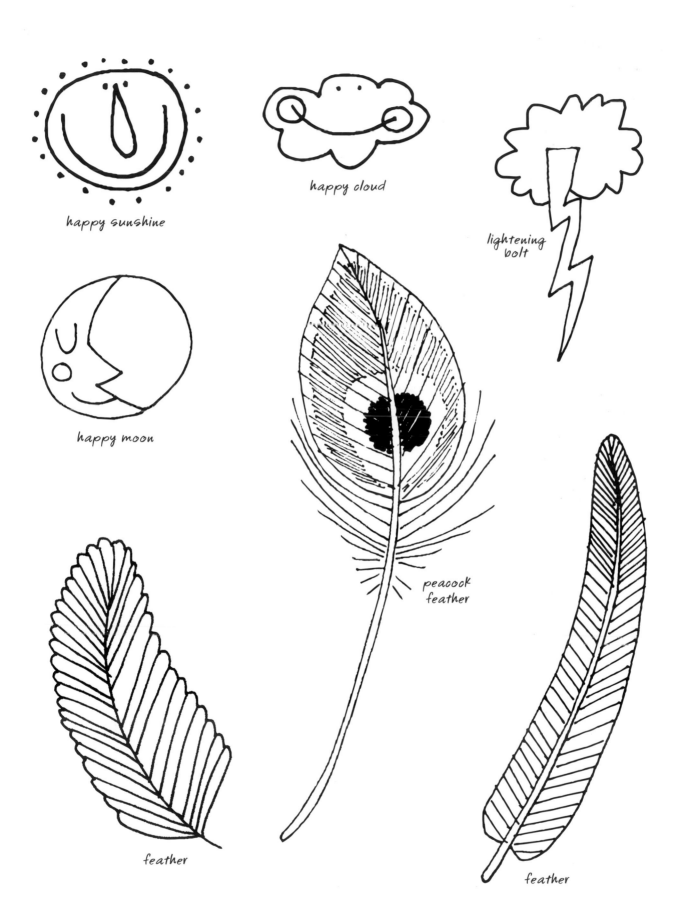

happy sunshine

happy cloud

lightening bolt

happy moon

peacock feather

feather

feather

matches

campfire match

bear head

rainbow

LATER
later gator

skinny acorn

band-aid

moose

deer

polka-dot thermos

camping thermos

fat acorn

BON VOYAGE!

bon voyage lettering

suitcase

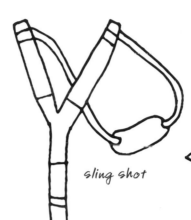

sling shot

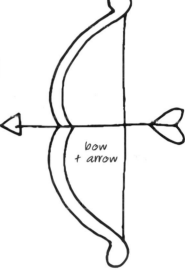

bow + arrow

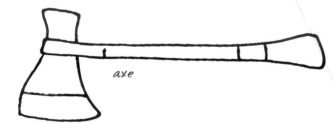

axe

dragonfly

bees

butterfly

mountain scene

star patch

tent patch

bear-paw patch

heart patch

tree patch

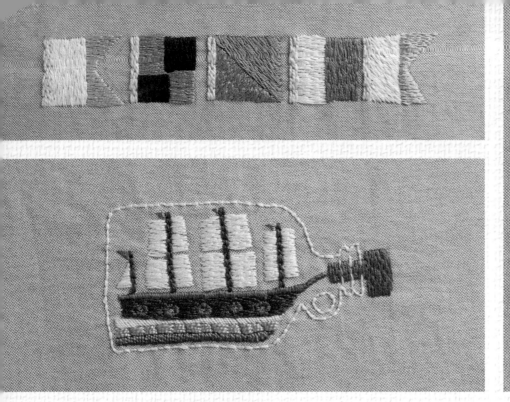

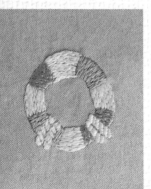

By the Sea

ship in a bottle

sailboat

sunfish / small sailboat

happy submarine

trolling boat

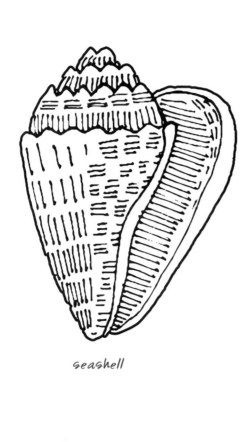

seashell

pearl in a clam

monkey's fist

conch shell

seashell

squished starfish

starfish

grog

sunscreen

swim trunks

bikini

life saver

bucket of sand

sunset polaroid

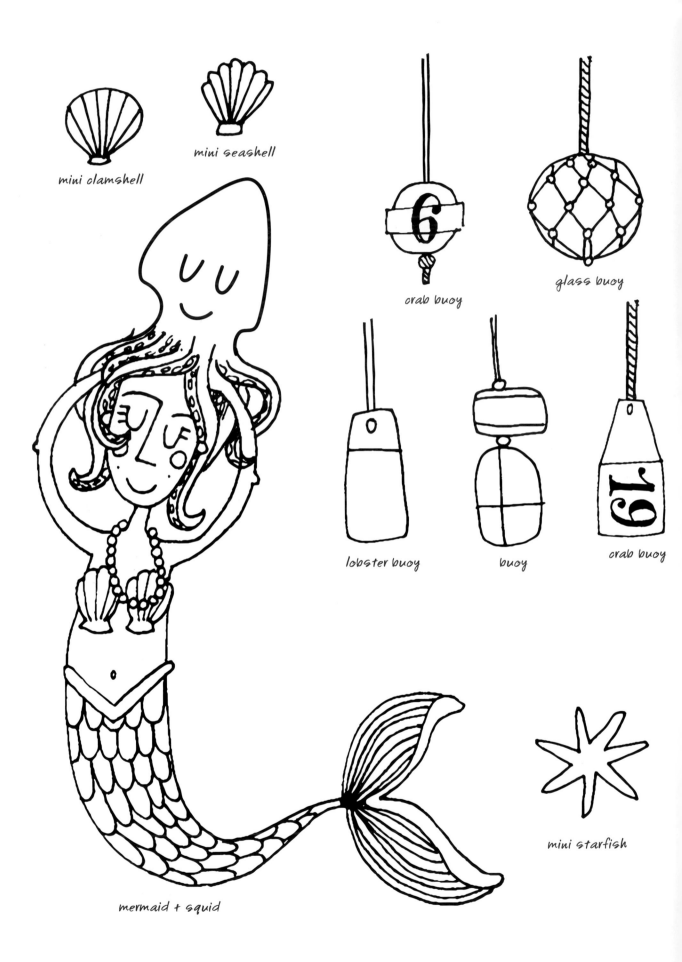

mini clamshell

mini seashell

crab buoy

glass buoy

lobster buoy

buoy

crab buoy

mermaid + squid

mini starfish

beach hat

sand crab

hermit crab

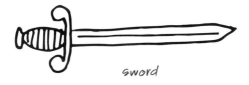

sword

dolphin circle

school of fish

beach umbrella

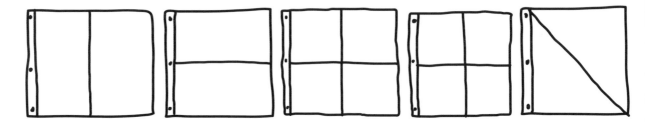

nautical flags

pigeon + coconut

anchor

beach palm tree

palm tree

lighthouse

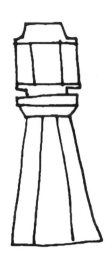

lighthouse

lighthouse

loch ness monster

conch

mini conch

ahoy lettering

lion

zebra

quail

panda + bamboo

squirrel

bunny

moth

cardinal

butterfly

porcupine

butterfly

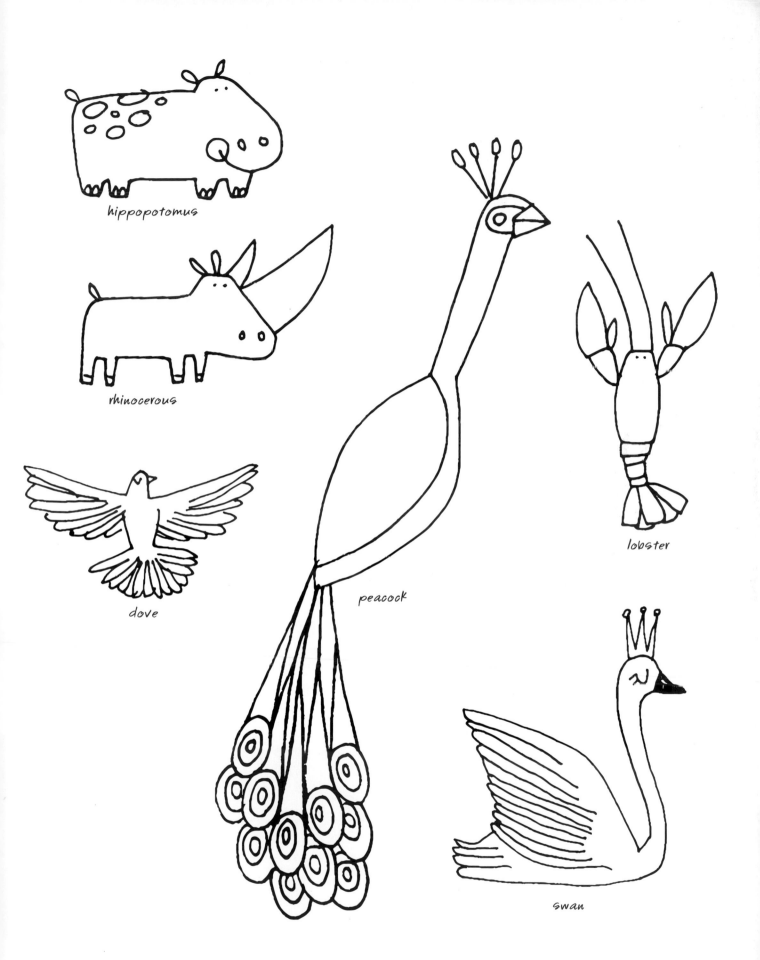

hippopotomus

rhinocerous

dove

peacock

lobster

swan

coiled snake

shark

turtle

triceratops

brontosaurus

stegasaurus

mutt / dog

common dog

chihuahua

poodle

fluffy dog

fluffy dog

dachshund

dalmation

WOOF

woof lettering

cat

meow

meow lettering

reindeer

unicorn

pig

bat

mini dog

mini turtle

mini dinosaur

mini cat face

mini ant

blue crab

flamingo

penguin

leopard

giraffe + mouse

Plants

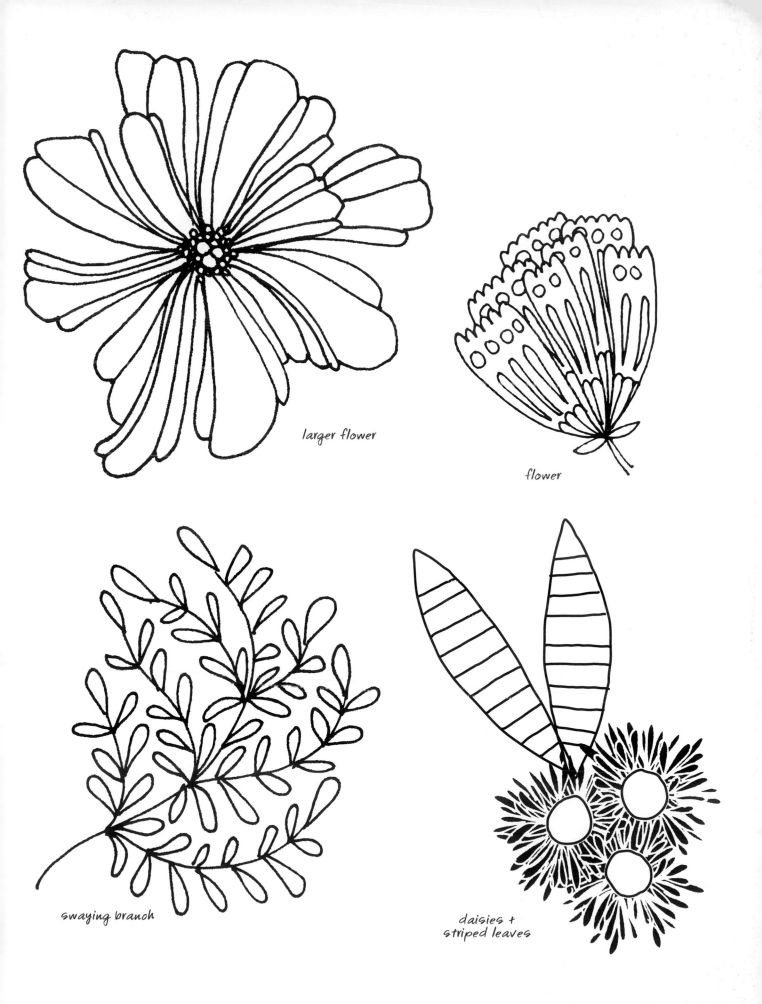

larger flower

flower

swaying branch

daisies +
striped leaves

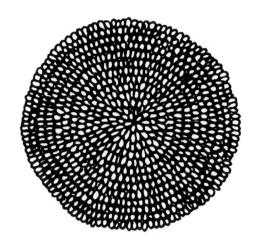

seeds

leaf + berries

flower cluster

flower burst

flower

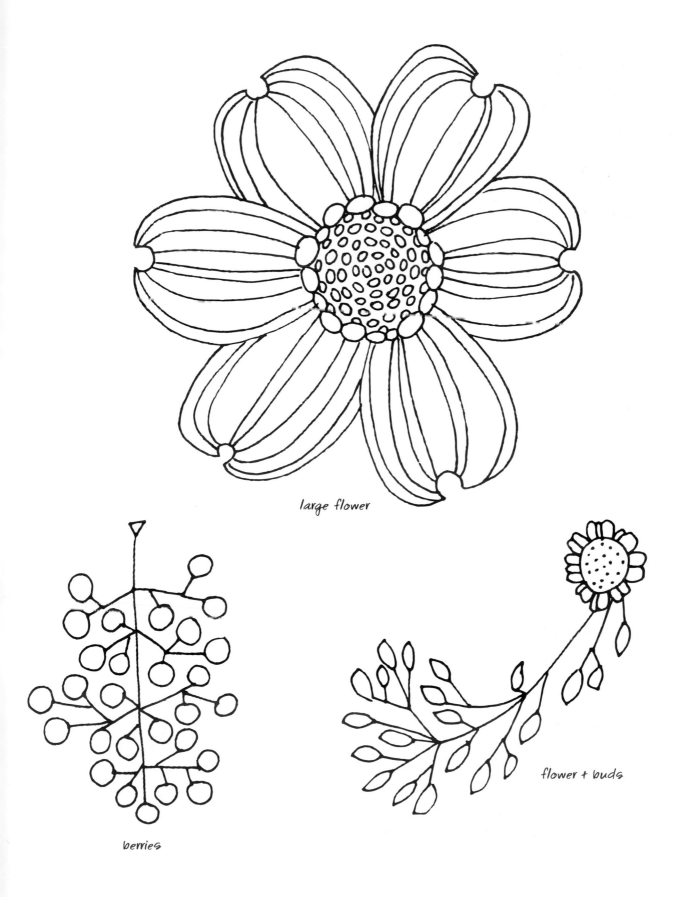

large flower

berries

flower + buds

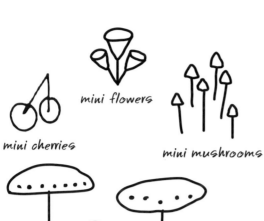

mini flowers

mini cherries

mini mushrooms

flowers

mini mushrooms

olive branch

flowers

flower + leaf

daisy

tropical leaf

floral burst

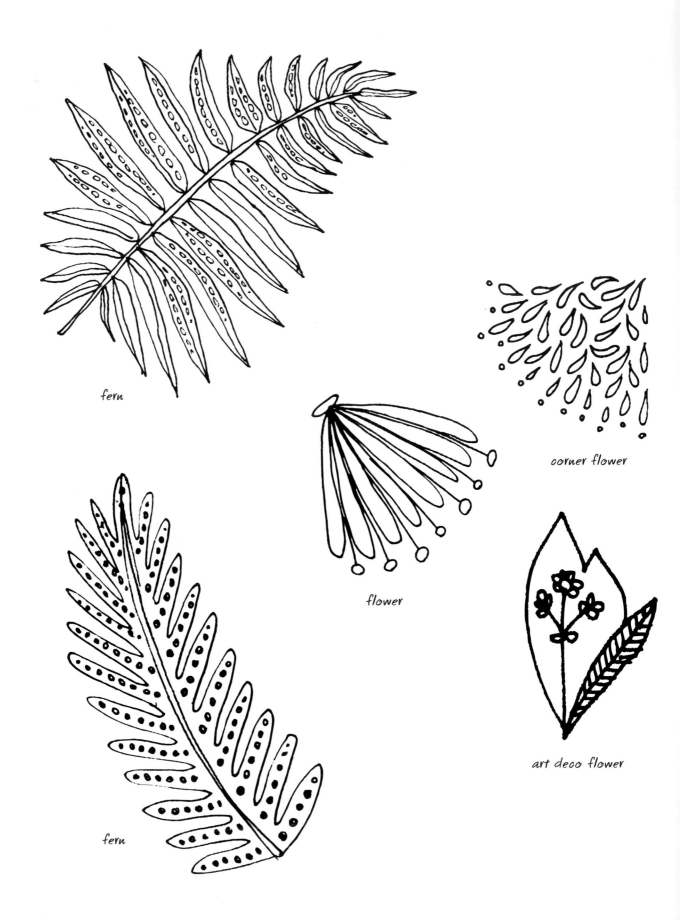

fern

corner flower

flower

art deco flower

fern

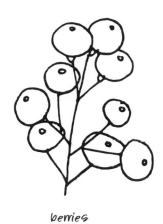

berries

sprig

bouquet of
weeds

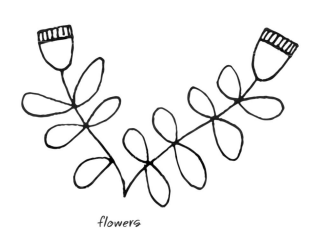

flowers

flower

bluebells

floral branch
+ leaf

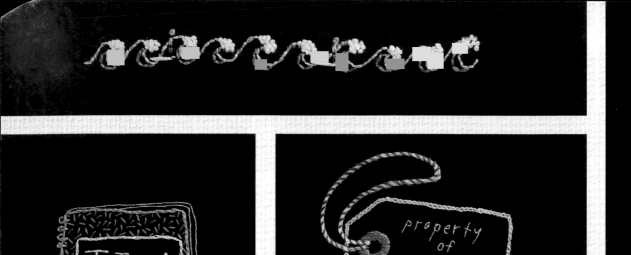

TIM

property of anne

Frames & Borders

a GIFT for my BEST FRIEND 2015

TO

FROM

T · S

WATS

est. · 2011

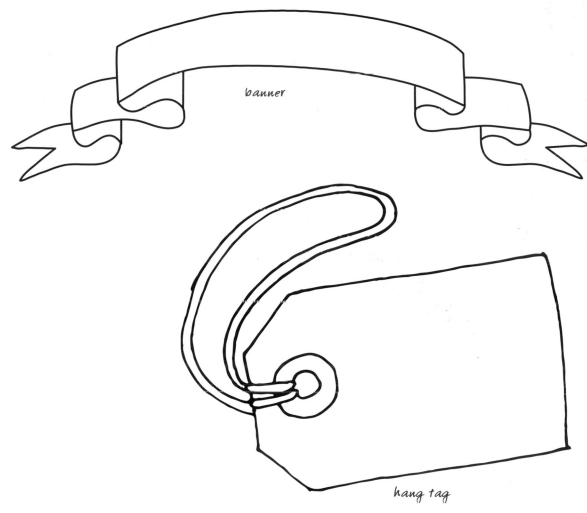

banner

hang tag

THINGS I LOVE

1. _____

2. _____

3. _____

4. _____

5 _____

list frame

sunburst frame

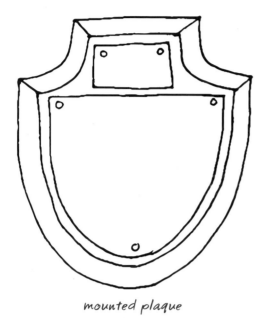

mounted plaque

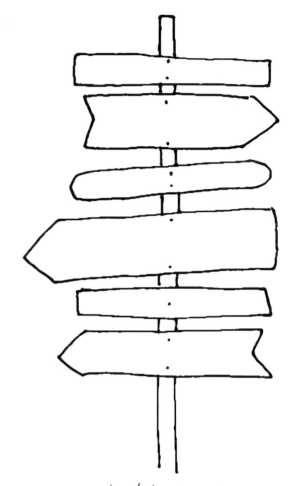

beach-town arrows

woven frame

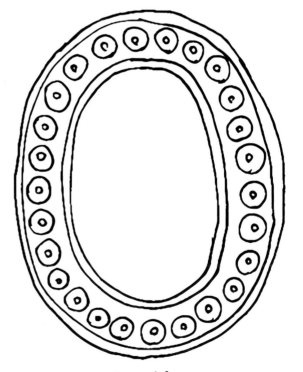

sequin oval frame

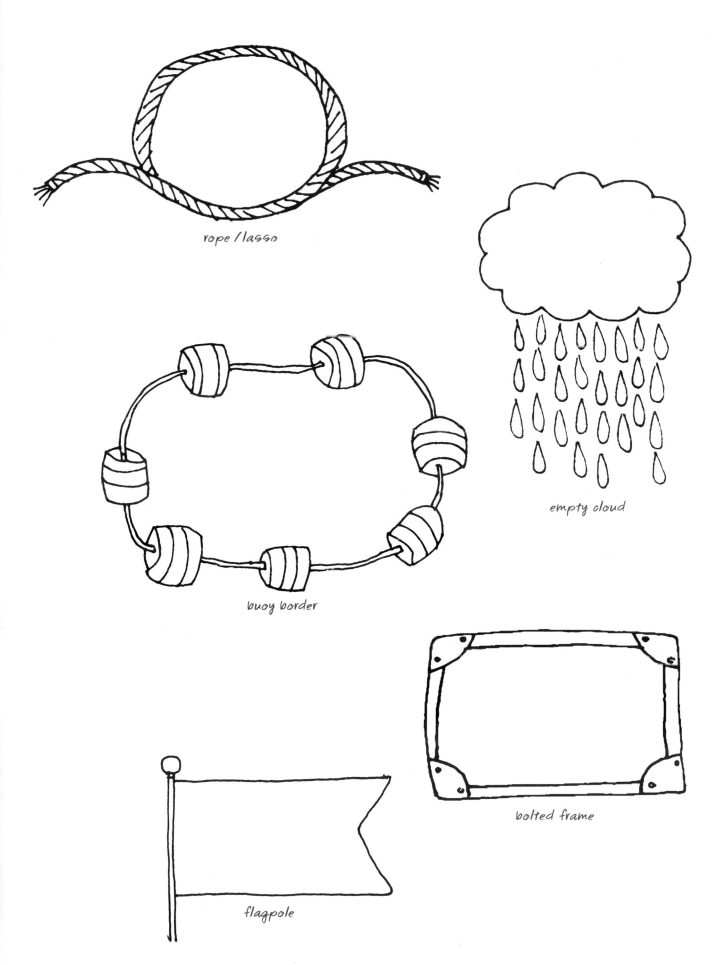

rope / lasso

empty cloud

buoy border

bolted frame

flagpole

camp sign

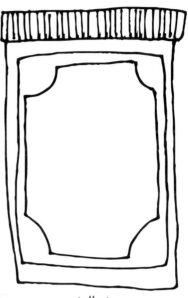

jelly jar

spiral notebook

floral frame

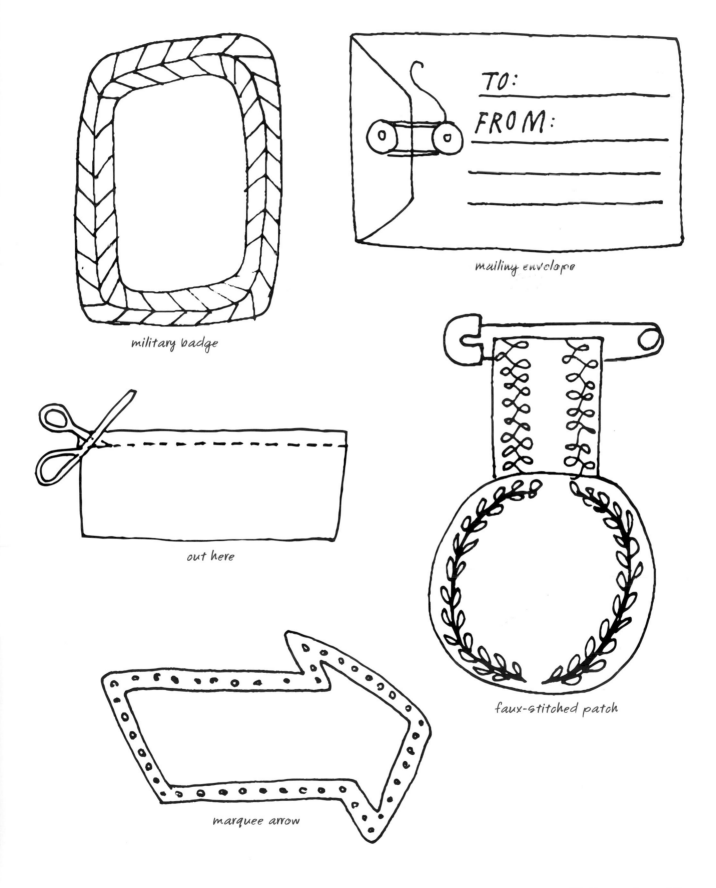

military badge

mailing envelope

TO:

FROM:

out here

faux-stitched patch

marquee arrow

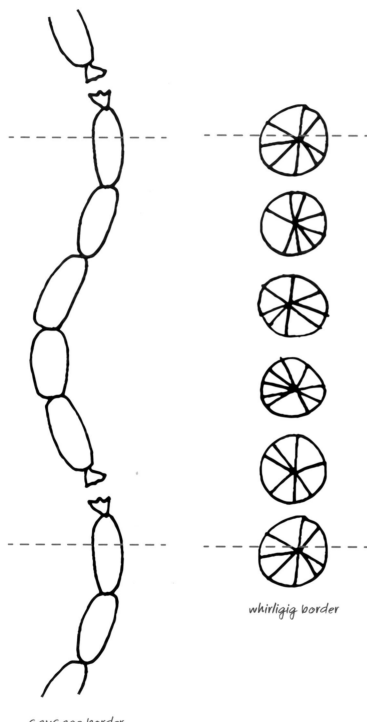

sausage border

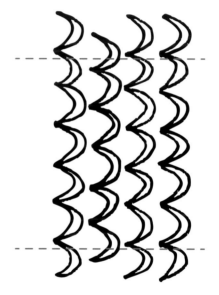

whirligig border

waves border

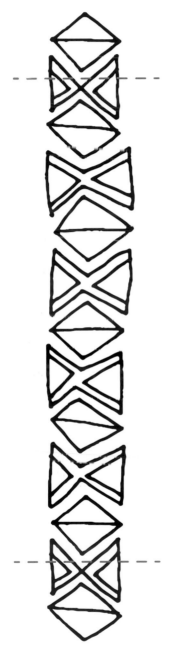

aztec border

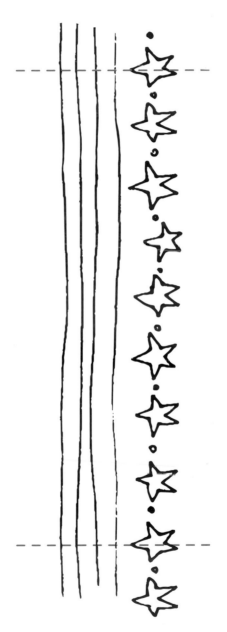

stars and stripes border

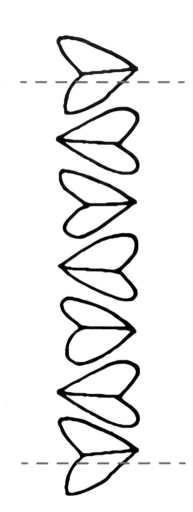

heart border

Kitchen border

rope border

rope border

festive floral border

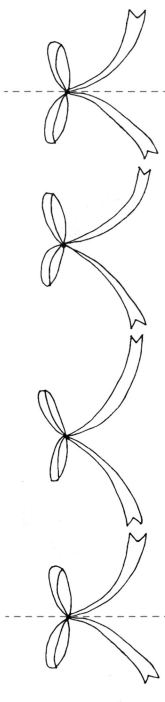

bows border

ribbon border

sunny-day border

threaded border

folk floral border

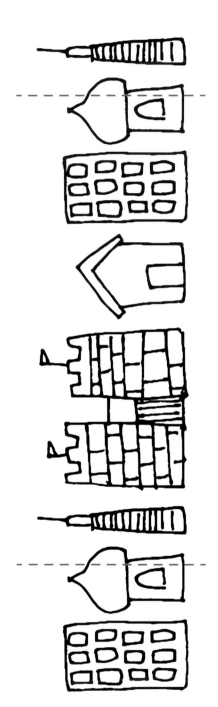

homes border

citrus border

toes-to-the-nose border

Alphabets

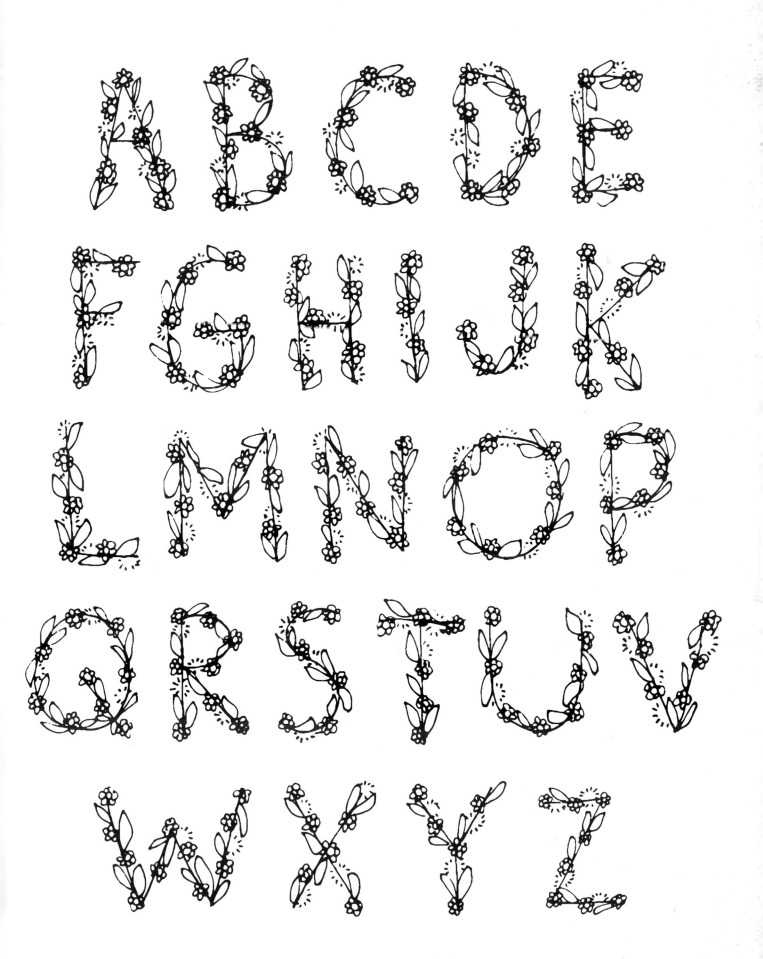

A B C D E F
G H I J K L
M N O P Q R
S T U V W
X Y Z

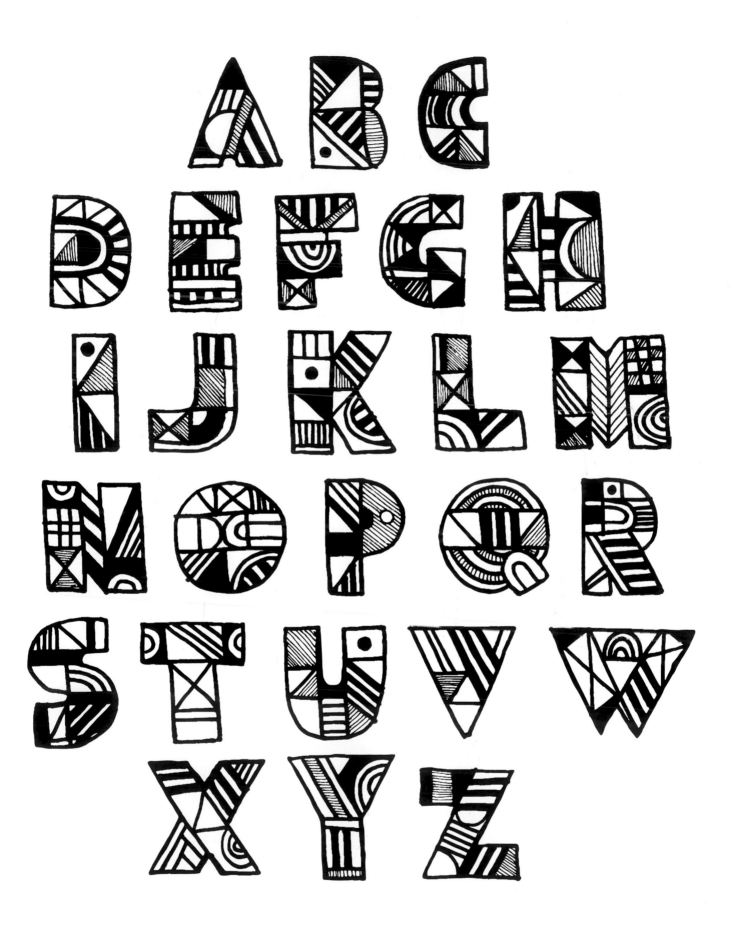

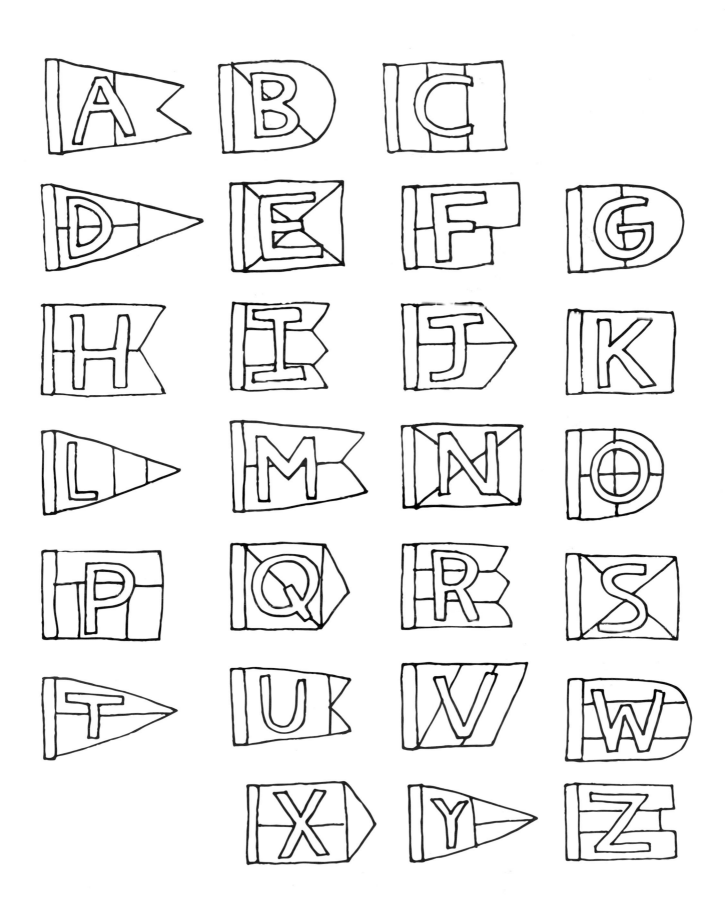

Resources

FOR EMBROIDERY SUPPLIES

Aurifil

www.aurifil.com

Aurifil is a manufacturer of fine sewing, quilting, and embroidery threads.

DMC

www.dmc.com

DMC offers embroidery floss, yarns, and other needlecraft supplies, as well as tips and tutorials.

Purl Soho

www.purlsoho.com

Purl Soho is a New York City store that also has a wonderful online shop where you can find a wide variety of fine threads, base cloths, and needlework accessories.

Westminster Fibers

www.westminsterfibers.com

http://www.westminster fibers.com/pdf/AnchortoDM Cconversion.pdf

This website offers a variety of embroidery floss and yarns. In addition, you can use it to find and compare threads of a particular color across a variety of different brands.

FOR EMBROIDERY TIPS + INSTRUCTION IN A WIDE VARIETY OF STITCHES

The Embroidery Stitch Bible by Betty Barnden. Krause Publications, 2003.

DMC Creative World

www.dmc-usa.com/Education/Technique-Overviews/Embroidery.aspx

For information about cutting skeins of embroidery threads, click on Getting Ready, under How to Embroider.

Mary Corbet's Needle 'N Thread

www.needlenthread.com/ tips-techniques

materialistic

http://kellyfletcher.blogspot.com br/p/stitch-directory.html

About the CD

SYSTEM REQUIREMENTS

PDF viewer application

Although it is recommended that you use Adobe Acrobat Reader 9 to view the disk content, your computer may be set up to open PDF files in a different application by default. If your computer does not have an application to view PDF files, you can get the latest version of the free Adobe Acrobat Reader from the Adobe website: http://get.adobe.com/reader/. Simply copy this URL and paste it into your browser's address bar.

Windows

Intel® 1.3GHz or faster processor

Microsoft® Windows® XP Home, Professional, or Tablet PC Edition with Service Pack 3 (32 bit) or Service Pack 2 (64 bit)

Windows Server® 2003 (with Service Pack 2 for 64 bit)

Windows Server® 2008 (32 bit and 64 bit)

Windows Server 2008 R2 (32 bit and 64 bit)

Windows Vista® Home Basic, Home Premium, Business, Ultimate, or Enterprise with Service Pack 2

(32 bit and 64 bit)

Microsoft Windows 7 or Windows 7 with Service Pack

1 Starter, Home Premium, Professional, Ultimate, or Enterprise (32 bit and 64 bit)

256MB of RAM (512MB recommended)

260MB of available hard-disk space

Color monitor of at least 1024x576 screen resolution

Internet Explorer 7, 8 or 9, Firefox 3.6, 4.0 or 6.0, Chrome 9.0

Mac OS

Intel processor

Mac OS X 10.5.8 or 10.6.8 or 10.7.x

512MB of RAM (1G recommended)

415MB of available hard-disk space

Color monitor of at least 800x600 screen resolution (1024x768 recommended)

Apple Safari 4 for Mac OS X 10.5.8 and Mac OS X

10.6.7 Safari 5 for Mac OS X 10.6.7—10.6.8

Viewing the Content

1 Once you've inserted the CD into your CD-ROM drive, a window should open displaying the contents of the disk. If a window does not open, navigate to the CD drive and open the disk manually. On Windows, you can do this by going to My Computer and selecting the CD. On the Mac, double-click on the CD icon on the Desktop.

2 The contents of the CD are organized according to the chapters in this book. Simply open the chapter folder where the motif is found in the book and double-click the motif you need. For example, FOOD contains all the food-related motifs. Open the FOOD folder, double-click the Ice Cream Cone, and the motif is available to print.

3 Print the motif at 100% or resize to fit your project.

Index

Published by Interweave, an imprint of F+W, A Content + eCommerce Company, 10151 Carver Road, Suite 200, Blue Ash, Ohio 45242. (800) 289-0963. First Edition.

a content + ecommerce company

www.fwcommunity.com

19 18 17 16 15   5 4 3 2 1

Distributed in Canada by Fraser Direct
100 Armstrong Avenue
Georgetown, ON, Canada L7G 5S4
Tel: (905) 877-4411

Distributed in the U.K. and Europe by F&W MEDIA
INTERNATIONAL
Brunel House, Newton Abbot, Devon, TQ12 4PU, England
Tel: (+44) 1626 323200, Fax: (+44) 1626 323319
E-mail: enquiries@fwmedia.com

Distributed in Australia by Capricorn Link
P.O. Box 704, S. Windsor NSW, 2756 Australia
Tel: (02) 4560 1600, Fax: (02) 4577 5288
E-mail: books@capricornlink.com.au

SRN: 15SW02
ISBN-13: 978-1-62033-952-7

PDF SRN: EP9452
PDF ISBN-13: 978-1-62033-953-4

Editor Cynthia Bix

Technical Editor Kerry Smith

Photographer Donald Scott

Cover + Interior Design Pamela Norman

Acknowledgments

Many thanks go out to my entire family, who are always excited and enthusiastic to hear about my work. I am so lucky to have such a great support network. To my parents, first a big hug, and also, thanks. I never would have realized my creativity if I didn't have you two as perfect examples, showing me the way. And thanks especially to my husband, who supports me in every way, and never complains about fabric and thread all over the house. I love you all.

ABOUT THE AUTHOR

Sarah Watson is an illustrator, embroiderer, wife, and mother. She has illustrated children's books and designed fabric collections, and she creates patterns for a variety of products. She loves to draw and create, and if you happen to find her, you will probably see her hands busy with an embroidery or illustration. Sarah grew up in Alabama and now lives in Brazil. You can find her online at sarahwatsonillustration.com.

Sew much fun to be had —where will you start?